CONTENTS

INTRODUCTION

This book is designed to serve a variety of needs and interests for teachers, students, parents, and tutors. The contents of this book are based upon both state and national standards. Teachers can use this book for review and remediation. Students will find the content to be concise and focused on the major concepts of the discipline. Parents can use this book to help their children with topics that may be posing a problem in the classroom. Tutors can use the material as a basis for their lessons and for assigning problems and questions.

Each unit follows the same sequence in covering a major topic. Each unit opens with *Key Terms*, which include all the boldfaced terms and their definitions presented in the same order as they are introduced in the text. As a result, the reader can develop a sense of the topics that are covered in the unit. The unit follows with a clear and concisely written *text*, which is divided into several sections. Each section is written so that the reader is not overwhelmed with details but rather guided through the topic in a logical sequence. Each unit then moves on to a *Review*, which consists of several multiple-choice and short-answer questions. The questions follow the same sequence as the material presented in the unit. As a result, the reader can easily locate the section where a review may be needed. Each unit concludes with a series of *activities*. These activities are designed to assess the reader's understanding of the content and to apply the information learned to novel situations. As a change of pace, some of the activities are meant to engage the reader in a "fun-type" exercise using a crossword puzzle or other similar device as a way of reinforcing the content. The book concludes with a *Glossary*, which lists all the boldfaced terms in alphabetical order, and an *Answer Key*, which gives the answers to all the activity questions.

This book has been designed and written so that teachers, students, parents, and tutors will all find it easy to use and follow. Most importantly, students will benefit from this book by achieving at a higher level in class and on standardized tests.

Cells

All **organisms**, or living things, are made of one or more **cells**. A cell is the smallest unit of a living thing that can carry on all the processes of life. Microscopic observations of living things led to the development of the cell theory. This theory has three parts:

1. All organisms are composed of one or more cells.
2. The cell is the basic unit of structure and function in an organism.
3. All cells arise from preexisting cells.

The origin of the cell theory can be traced back to Robert Hooke (1635–1703). Hooke used a microscope to examine a thin slice of cork. He saw tiny structures that he called "little boxes" that reminded him of the cells in which monks lived. So Hooke called these structures cells. What Hooke had actually seen were the remains of dead plant cells. In addition to Hooke, other scientists made observations that led to the development of the cell theory.

Key Terms

organism—a living thing

cell—the smallest unit of a living thing that can carry on all the processes of life

organelle—a cell component that performs a specific function

prokaryote—a single-celled organism with only one organelle, a cell membrane

eukaryote—a cell that contains a cell membrane, a nucleus, and other organelles

cytoplasm—the part of a cell between the nucleus and the cell membrane

binary fission—the process where a prokaryotic cell splits to form two cells

mitosis—the process of cell division in eukaryotic cells

meiosis—the process of cell division which forms mature sex cells

haploid—the chromosome number in a mature sex cell

diploid—the chromosome number in most cells of an organism

crossing-over—the process in meiosis where chromosomes exchange genetic information

homeostasis—the process where a cell or organism maintains a stable internal environment

diffusion—the movement of substances from an area of high concentration to an area of lower concentration

osmosis—the movement of water molecules across a membrane from an area of higher concentration to an area of lower concentration

solute—a substance that dissolves in a solution

hypotonic—of two solutions, the solution with a lower solute concentration

hypertonic—of two solutions, the solution with a higher solute concentration

isotonic—the condition in which the concentration of solutes outside a cell equals the concentration inside the cell

Animal Cells

Cells exist in a wide variety of shapes and sizes. Some cells are very simple in structure, while others are much more complex. These more complex cells contain various internal structures called **organelles**. An organelle is a cell component that performs a specific function.

The simplest cells contain only one organelle. These simple cells are called **prokaryotes**. Bacteria are classified as prokaryotes, which are single-celled organisms. The only organelle that prokaryotes possess is a cell membrane. A cell membrane is the structure that surrounds a cell and controls what enters and leaves. Organisms whose cells contain a cell membrane and other organelles are called **eukaryotes.** Eukaryotes are organisms made of many cells and include both animals and plants.

Animal cells come in a wide variety of shapes and sizes. Many animal cells are also specialized to perform a specific function. Nonetheless, certain organelles are common to almost all animal cells. The following figure illustrates the organelles commonly found in animal cells.

The following table lists the various organelles and their functions. The organelles between the nucleus and the cell membrane are located in the **cytoplasm** of a cell.

Organelle	Function
Cell membrane	controls what enters and leaves the cell
Nucleus	contains the genetic information and directs most of the cell's activities
Mitochondrion	supplies the energy needed by the cell
Ribosome	organizes the synthesis of proteins
Rough endoplasmic reticulum	prepares proteins for export by the cell
Smooth endoplasmic reticulum	synthesizes steroids, regulates calcium levels, and breaks down toxic substances
Golgi apparatus	prepares proteins for secretion by the cell
Lysosome	contains digestive enzymes
Microfilaments and microtubules	contribute to cell support, movement, and division

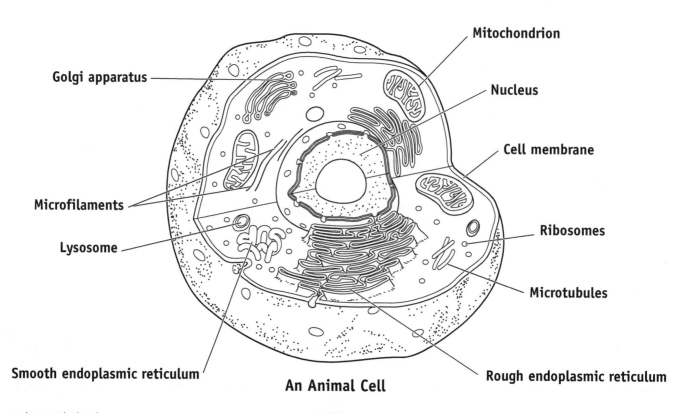

An Animal Cell

Unit 1, Cells
Biology, SV 0423-9

Plant Cells

Most of the organelles just described are common to all eukaryotic cells, including plant cells. However, plant cells have three additional organelles not found in animal cells. These organelles are important to the functions of a plant cell. The following figure illustrates the organelles found in plant cells.

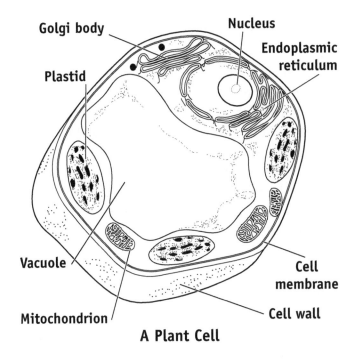

A Plant Cell

One organelle is a cell wall, which lies outside the cell membrane. A cell wall is made of long chains of cellulose, a carbohydrate. The cellulose makes the cell wall rigid, providing support and protection for the plant cell.

Another organelle in plant cells is a vacuole. This organelle stores water, enzymes, and waste products. The vacuole inside a plant cell may be so large that it pushes the other organelles up against the cell membrane.

The third organelle found in a plant cell is a plastid. Some plastids store starch or fats. Other plastids contain a pigment, which absorbs visible light. The most familiar plastid is a chloroplast, which contains a green pigment called chlorophyll. Chloroplasts contain large amounts of chlorophyll, giving leaves their green color. Other types of plastids contain different pigments, such as orange and red. These pigments are masked by the chlorophyll until cooler weather arrives in the fall.

Mitosis

According to the cell theory, all cells come from preexisting cells. Therefore, cells must divide to produce new cells. Prokaryotic cells divide by a process called **binary fission**. At the start of this process, the chromosome, which contains the genetic information, makes a copy of itself. Next, the prokaryotic cell grows until it is almost twice its original size. Finally, the cell splits into two cells, each containing a complete chromosome.

Cell division in eukaryotic cells is more complicated. The process of cell division in eukaryotic cells is called **mitosis**. Mitosis is the process where a cell divides to produce two cells that contain the identical genetic information as found in the original cell. Mitosis is a division of the nucleus. Although this division of the nucleus is a continuous process, mitosis is divided into four phases. Each phase has unique characteristics.

In prophase, the first stage of mitosis, the chromosomes become visible by shortening and coiling. In the second phase, metaphase, the chromosomes align themselves in the middle of the dividing cell. In anaphase, the third phase, each member of a chromosome pair separates and begins to move toward the opposite end of the cell. In the fourth and final phase, telophase, the cell begins to divide into two new cells as the chromosomes reach opposite ends of the cell. An animal cell undergoes telophase by forming a furrow that pinches in the cell membrane. A plant cell undergoes telophase by forming a new cell wall called a cell plate. Once mitosis is complete, the two new cells enter interphase, where they spend most of their lifetime. Interphase is the stage where each chromosome makes a copy of itself.

Meiosis

Mature reproductive cells do not form by mitosis. Rather they form by a process called **meiosis**. Meiosis is a process which reduces the chromosome number in new cells to half the number present in the original cell. For example, in humans, meiosis produces reproductive cells, called gametes, that each contain 23 chromosomes. This number of chromosomes represents the **haploid** number in human gametes.

Therefore, a mature sperm and egg each contain a haploid number, or 23 chromosomes. When a sperm fertilizes an egg, the result in humans is 46 chromosomes. This number represents the **diploid** number in human cells.

Like mitosis, meiosis begins with interphase where each chromosome makes a copy. From this point, however, the process of meiosis is more complicated than mitosis. First, unlike mitosis, which involves one division, meiosis involves two divisions—meiosis I and meiosis II. During meiosis I, chromosomes break apart and exchange genetic material with one another. This process is called **crossing-over**, which produces a new mixture of genetic material. Meiosis I results in two cells, each of which has half the chromosome number. However, each chromosome still exists in two copies. Each copy separates during meiosis II. As a result of meiosis I and meiosis II, four mature gametes are produced, each containing the haploid number of chromosomes. In addition, each gamete contains a chromosome combination that differs from the original cell because of crossing-over.

Diffusion and Osmosis

To stay alive and functioning, all cells must maintain a stable internal environment despite changes in their external environment. This process of maintaining a stable internal environment is called **homeostasis**. One way cells maintain homeostasis is by controlling what substances may enter or leave. This function is carried out by the cell membrane.

The simplest way substances move across a cell membrane is by **diffusion**. Diffusion is the movement of substances from an area of higher concentration to an area of lower concentration. Diffusion results in a situation where the concentration of a substance is the same throughout a space.

For example, consider what happens if a cell becomes surrounded by a fluid that contains a higher salt concentration than is found inside the cell. The salt will diffuse into the cell until the concentration inside the cell equals the concentration outside the cell. Substances that are very small, like salt, can diffuse through a cell membrane by passing through its pores. Substances that dissolve in lipids can also diffuse through a cell membrane because it is made partly of lipids.

Water can diffuse across a cell membrane. The diffusion of water across a cell membrane is called **osmosis**. Like diffusion, osmosis involves movement from an area of higher concentration to an area of lower concentration. Consider a situation where the concentration of water molecules is higher outside a cell. In this situation, the concentration of other substances, such as salt and sugar, is higher inside the cell.

When dissolved in water, salt and sugar are known as **solutes**. When the concentration of solutes inside a cell is higher than the concentration outside the cell, the solution outside is said to be **hypotonic** to the cell. In this situation, water moves by osmosis from outside to inside the cell. To survive and maintain homeostasis, a cell may have to get rid of the water entering by osmosis. Some single-celled organisms eliminate water with the help of special organelles that collect and then pump out the water.

When the concentration of solutes inside a cell is lower than the concentration outside the cell, the solution outside is said to be **hypertonic** to the cell. In this situation, water moves by osmosis from inside to the outside of the cell. This is what happens when a plant begins to wilt when it is not watered.

Some cells have no mechanism for maintaining homeostasis in either a hypotonic or hypertonic environment. For example, human red blood cells will swell and burst in a hypotonic environment and shrivel and die in a hypertonic environment. As a result, these cells must remain in an environment where the water concentration is balanced inside and outside the cell. This is known as an **isotonic** environment. Fortunately, the human body has various mechanisms for maintaining the water concentration of the liquid portion of the blood so that it is isotonic to red blood cells.

UNIT 1

Review

Darken the circle by the best answer.

1. Which organelle is found in all cells?

   (Ⓐ) nucleus

   (B) cytoplasm

   → (C) cell membrane

   (D) rough endoplasmic reticulum

2. Which organelle is found in both animal and plant cells?

   (A) vacuole

   (Ⓑ) endoplasmic reticulum

   (C) plastid

   (D) cell wall

3. Proteins are synthesized on the

   (Ⓐ) ribosomes.

   (B) mitochondria.

   (C) cell membrane.

   (D) cell wall.

4. As a result of mitosis,

   (A) the chromosome number is reduced by half.

   (B) new chromosome combinations are formed.

   (Ⓒ) two cells are produced that contain the same number and kinds of chromosomes as the original cell.

   (D) each cell formed has new genetic information.

5. Which process occurs during meiosis?

   (A) return to the diploid condition

   (Ⓑ) crossing-over

   (C) formation of a new cell wall

   (D) change from the haploid number of chromosomes to the diploid number

6. If a cell is placed in a hypotonic environment, the cell will

   (Ⓐ) lose water and gain salts.

   → (B) gain water and lose salts.

   (C) lose both water and salts.

   (D) gain both water and salts.

7. A cell that is maintaining its internal water concentration is exhibiting

   (A) the final stages of mitosis.

   (B) a loss of water molecules.

   (C) a higher salt concentration than its environment.

   (Ⓓ) homeostasis.

→ 8. Identify two organelles you would expect to find highly concentrated in a cell that produces a lot of proteins.

   Vecuole, Mitochondrion?

9. Describe two ways in which mitosis differs from meiosis.

   Me: Divides & forms.

   Mi: Divides.

UNIT 1

Animal and Plant Cells

Match the function in column I with the organelle or structure in column II. A function in column I may match more than one item listed in column II. Also, an item in column II can be used more than once.

Column I

1. contains the hereditary information ___C___

2. provides energy to a cell ___G___

3. digests molecules and old organelles ___H___

4. supports and protects the cell ___K___

5. synthesizes steroids ___J___

6. controls what enters a cell ___B___

7. organizes the synthesis of proteins ___E___

8. stores pigments ___M___

9. stores waste products ___A___

10. directs the cell's activities ___C___

11. contributes to cell movement ___D___

12. prepares proteins for cell export ___I___

13. packages substances produced by the cell ___F___

14. controls what leaves the cell ___B___

15. made of cellulose ___K___

Column II

A. vacuole

B. cell membrane

C. nucleus

D. microfilament

E. Golgi apparatus

F. chromosome

G. mitochondrion

H. lysosome

I. rough endoplasmic reticulum

J. smooth endoplasmic reticulum

K. cell wall

L. ribosome

M. plastid

Unit 1, Cells
Biology, SV 0423-9

Animal and Plant Cells (cont'd.)

Choose the term that does not belong to each of the following groups and explain your choice.

16. plastid, ~~chloroplast~~, mitochondrion, pigment

It's not in either of the pictures of cells.

_____

17. ribosome, ~~cell wall~~, nucleus, cell membrane

Not in animal cell.

_____

18. ~~chromosome~~, Golgi apparatus, smooth endoplasmic reticulum, lysosome

Not in animal cell.

_____

Answer the following questions.

19. Would you expect a muscle cell to have many or few mitochondria? Explain your answer.

Many. I saw 3 in animal cell picture, pg. 4.

_____

_____

20. Explain why a plant cell is classified as a eukaryotic cell.

A eukaryotic has a cell membrene, nucleus & other organelles. Plant cells have that stuff.

UNIT 1

Mitosis

Examine the following illustrations of the four phases of mitosis. Name each phase. Describe the major features that are characteristic of each stage. Note that the phases are not shown in the correct order they follow in mitosis. Number the order in which they occur.

1.

phase _Anaphase_

order _3_

features _They start to separate_

2.

phase _Prophase_

order _1_

features _Shortening & coiling_

3.

phase _Metaphase_

order _2_

features _They align themselves in the middle of the dividing cell._

4.

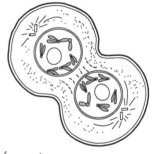

phase _Telophase_

order _4_

features _Throughout the 4 phases, the cell is slowly dividing itself._

UNIT 1

Mitosis and Meiosis

Both mitosis and meiosis involve cell division. However, they have distinct differences. Determine whether the following features apply to mitosis, meiosis, or both by placing an X in the appropriate column.

Feature	Mitosis	Meiosis	Both
1. maintains diploid number of chromosomes	✓	✓	
2. involves crossing-over		✓	
3. chromosomes shorten and become visible	✓		
4. produces four cells when completed		✓	
5. involves only one division	✓		
6. reduces chromosome number		✓	
7. produces genetically identical cells	✓		
8. forms mature gametes		✓	✓
9. produces cells with new chromosome combinations			✓
10. occurs in animal cells	✓	✓	✓
11. occurs in plant cells			✓
12. forms skin cells			✓
13. involves chromosome movement			✓
14. goes through two divisions		✓	
15. produces haploid number		✓	
16. involves changes within the nucleus	✓		
17. produces two cells when completed	✓		
18. cell membrane pinches in	✓		

UNIT 1

Diffusion and Osmosis

> **Diffusion is the movement of substances from an area of higher concentration to an area of lower concentration. Osmosis is the diffusion of water through a membrane, such as a cell membrane.**

Use the following experimental set-up to answer the questions.

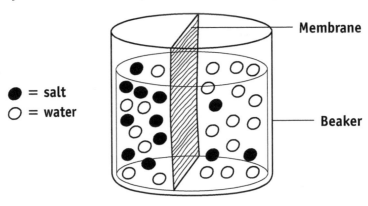

● = salt
○ = water

Membrane

Beaker

1. In which direction will salt move? Explain your answer.

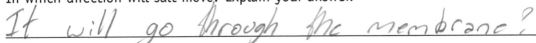 It will go through the membrane?

2. In which direction will water move? Explain your answer.

 From less concentate to more concentrate.

3. Redraw the above illustration to show what happens after diffusion and osmosis have occurred.

→  ←

4. Use the symbols above for salt and water to draw a cell in a hypotonic environment.

Every cell needs **energy** to carry on its functions. Energy is the capacity for doing work. You may think of a cell doing work when it moves or divides. Actually a cell needs energy to digest molecules, get rid of wastes, and synthesize substances. In fact, every life process is driven by energy. Taken together, all life processes are known as **metabolism**. Metabolism is the sum of all life processes occurring within an organism. These life processes involve a variety of chemical compounds. Most of these compounds are **organic compounds**, which are ones that are based on the element carbon. There are four principal kinds of organic compounds involved in metabolism. These include carbohydrates, lipids, proteins, and nucleic acids. The first three types of organic compounds will be covered in this unit, while the last type—nucleic acids—will be covered in a later unit.

Key Terms

energy—the capacity for doing work

metabolism—the sum of all life processes occurring within an organism

organic compound—a compound based on the element carbon

carbohydrate—a compound that is composed of carbon, hydrogen, and oxygen in the proportion of 1:2:1

polysaccharide—a large molecule made by linking many individual carbohydrates

lipid—a compound that is composed of a high proportion of carbon and hydrogen with a much smaller proportion of oxygen. Lipids include fats, oils, and waxes.

saturated fat—a lipid that contains only single bonds between its carbon atoms

unsaturated fat—a lipid that contains one or more double bonds between its carbon atoms

protein—a large molecule made from amino acids

amino acid—a molecule that is the building block of a protein

dehydration synthesis—the process of joining smaller molecules to form a larger one accompanied by the loss of a water molecule

polypeptide—a long chain of amino acids

enzyme—a chemical substance that speeds up the rate of a chemical reaction

respiration—a series of chemical reactions that break down organic compounds and transfer the energy they contain into a form that cells can use

Carbohydrates

A **carbohydrate** is a compound that is composed of the elements carbon, hydrogen, and oxygen in the proportion of 1:2:1. The general formula for a carbohydrate is $(CH_2O)_n$ where n represents the number of carbon atoms. For example, glucose, a carbohydrate that has six carbon atoms, has the formula $C_6H_{12}O_6$. Glucose plays a key role in storing energy in a cell.

Individual carbohydrates can be linked to form larger molecules called **polysaccharides.** Starch is a polysaccharide made by linking hundreds of glucose molecules. Other polysaccharides include glycogen, which animal cells use for energy, and cellulose, which plant cells use to construct their cell walls. The following figure illustrates how two carbohydrate molecules are linked. In this case, the product is called a disaccharide because it is made from two individual sugar molecules, or monosaccharides. Notice that a water molecule is also formed.

This process continues so that hundreds of glucose molecules are linked to form a polysaccharide. Besides glucose, other carbohydrates can be linked to form a variety of polysaccharides.

Key Terms cont'd.

ATP (adenosine triphosphate)—the main compound cells use for energy

glycolysis—the first pathway in respiration where glucose is changed into pyruvic acid

pyruvic acid—a key intermediate in respiration

fermentation—the pathway pyruvic acid follows in the absence of oxygen

anaerobic respiration—respiration without oxygen

aerobic respiration—respiration with oxygen

Krebs cycle—the second pathway in respiration, taken only if oxygen is available

electron transport chain—the third and final pathway in respiration, taken only if oxygen is available

heterotroph—an organism that obtains energy by eating other organisms

autotroph—an organism that converts light energy into chemical energy

photosynthesis—the process that converts light energy into chemical energy

Calvin cycle—the pathway in photosynthesis where carbon dioxide is changed into an organic compound

Lipids

A **lipid** is a compound that contains a high proportion of carbon and hydrogen compared to oxygen. An example of a lipid is a compound that has the formula $C_{57}H_{92}O_9$. Lipids include fats, oils, and waxes. Lipids are somewhat unusual in that they do not dissolve in water. In organisms, lipids store energy, serve as hormones, and are used to build cell membranes. Animal cell membranes contain a lipid called cholesterol.

Like polysaccharides, fats are built by joining smaller molecules. A fat consists of three fatty acids joined with one glycerol molecule. One such fatty acid is shown below.

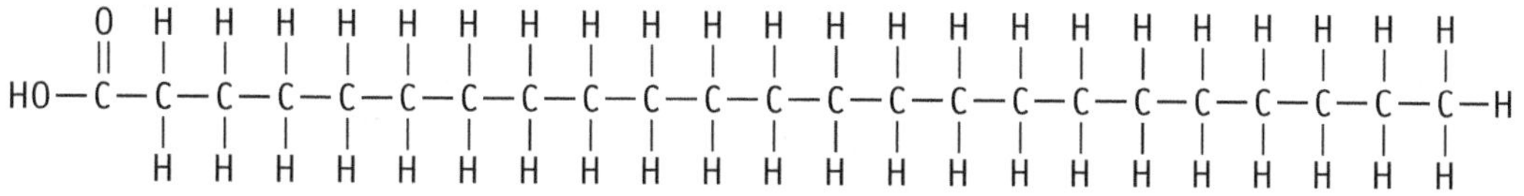

Each dash in the formula above represents a chemical bond. Notice that this fatty acid contains only a single dash, or a single bond, between the carbon atoms (C—C). This compound is part of a **saturated fat** where all the bonds between carbon atoms are single bonds. Contrast this to the fatty acid shown below.

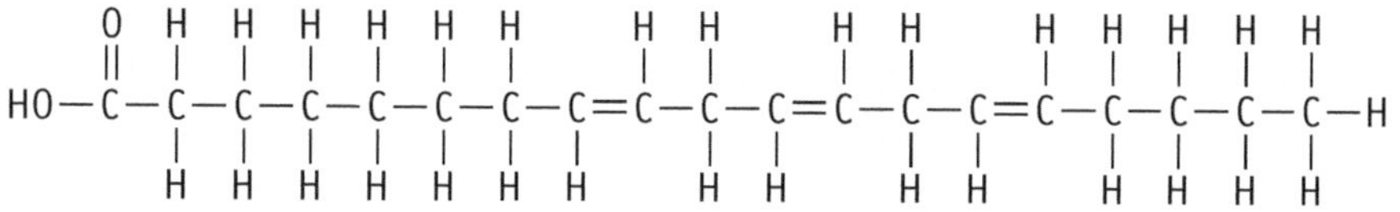

Notice that some of the bonds between carbon atoms in the formula above are double bonds, as shown by two dashes (C＝C). The formula above represents a fatty acid that is used to build an **unsaturated fat.** An unsaturated fat has at least one double bond between its carbon atoms. Nutritionists recommend that people try to eat foods that contain unsaturated fats, because consumption of saturated fats can lead to health problems, such as heart disease.

Proteins

A **protein** is a compound that consists of smaller molecules called **amino acids.** The following illustration shows how two amino acids are joined to form a larger molecule.

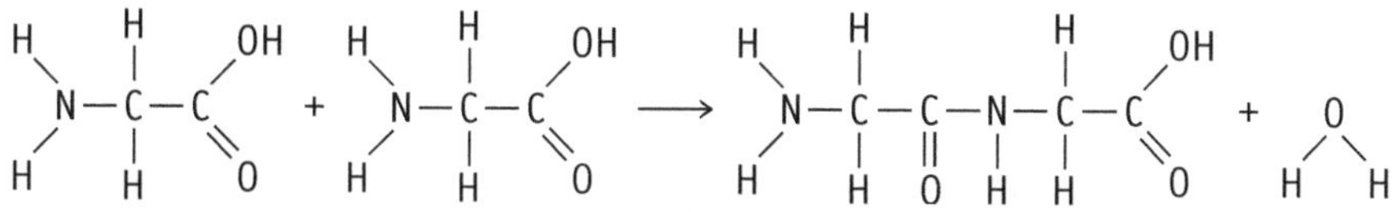

The link that connects two amino acids is called a peptide bond. Two amino acids that join form a dipeptide. Notice that an H was removed from one amino acid, while an OH was removed from the other amino acid. The H and OH combine to form water, H_2O. The process shown above is sometimes called **dehydration synthesis.**

The term *dehydration* comes from the water molecule that forms, while the term *synthesis* refers to the joining of smaller molecules to build a larger one. The process of dehydration synthesis continues so that hundreds of amino acids are linked to form a large molecule called a **polypeptide**. Several polypeptide chains are then joined and twisted to form a protein.

An important class of proteins includes **enzymes**. An enzyme is a chemical substance that speeds up the rate of a chemical reaction. Almost every chemical reaction that takes place in a cell depends upon an enzyme. A cell may contain thousands of different enzymes. Each enzyme is specific for a particular chemical reaction.

Respiration

Carbohydrates, lipids, and proteins are all involved in a process carried on by all cells. This process is **respiration**. Respiration is a series of chemical reactions that break down organic compounds and transfer the energy they contain into a compound that cells can use. The main compound cells use for energy is adenosine triphosphate, more commonly known by its abbreviation, **ATP**. ATP is the main energy currency of a cell. Respiration involves transferring the energy stored in organic compounds to ATP. The overall process of respiration involves several pathways. Each pathway consists of many steps.

Respiration begins with **glycolysis**. Many kinds of organic compounds are broken down in respiration. However, the carbohydrate glucose is typically used as the starting point. Glycolysis involves breaking down a six-carbon glucose molecule to form two three-carbon molecules called **pyruvic acid**. Two ATP molecules are needed to start glycolysis. However, four ATP molecules are made in the final step. As a result, glycolysis produces a net of two ATP molecules. However, much more energy remains stored in the pyruvic acid molecules.

What happens to pyruvic acid depends on whether or not oxygen is present. In the absence of oxygen, the process is known as **fermentation**. Pyruvic acid can follow one of two fermentation pathways. Yeast and some plant cells contain enzymes that change pyruvic acid into ethyl alcohol. This is known as alcoholic fermentation. Other cells, such as those that make up human muscles, contain different enzymes that change pyruvic acid into lactic acid. Too much lactic acid causes muscle fatigue and pain. No matter what the final product, fermentation does not produce any ATP. Because fermentation occurs in the absence of oxygen, it is referred to as **anaerobic respiration**.

Oxygen is needed to process pyruvic acid so that more ATP is made. In the presence of oxygen, pyruvic acid enters the pathways of **aerobic respiration**, or respiration that requires oxygen. The first pathway in aerobic respiration is the **Krebs cycle**. As its name suggests, the Krebs cycle ends where it starts. Each glucose molecule that is processed through the Krebs cycle produces only two ATP molecules. However, the Krebs cycle also produces hydrogen atoms. These hydrogen atoms will enter the next and final pathway of respiration.

This final pathway is known as the **electron transport chain**. Through a series of complex steps, hydrogen atoms are passed along the electron transport chain. As they do so, ATP is synthesized. Recall that before reaching the electron transport chain, only four ATP molecules have been made—two in glycolysis and two in the Krebs cycle. In contrast, the electron transport chain produces 34 ATP molecules for every glucose molecule that is processed. As a result, the respiration of one glucose molecule can generate up to 38 ATP molecules. However, oxygen is required to synthesize 34 of these 38 ATPs.

A common misconception about respiration is that oxygen turns into carbon dioxide. The fact is that oxygen turns into water as a result of aerobic respiration. The role of oxygen is simply to accept all the hydrogen atoms that are passed along the electron transport chain. By accepting these hydrogen atoms, oxygen turns into water, H_2O. The carbon dioxide that is produced by aerobic respiration comes from the Krebs cycle. This happens when a carbon atom and two oxygen atoms are removed from an organic compound in one of the steps of the Krebs cycle.

Photosynthesis

Some organisms obtain the energy they need from the organic materials they ingest. These organisms are called **heterotrophs**. Other organisms obtain the energy they need by manufacturing their own food. These organisms are called **autotrophs**. An autotroph converts light energy from the sun into chemical energy. Autotrophs store this chemical energy in various organic compounds, primarily carbohydrates. The process autotrophs use is **photosynthesis**.

Plants are the most common autotrophs that carry out photosynthesis. However, algae and some bacteria also carry out photosynthesis. Photosynthesis uses light energy to change carbon dioxide and water into oxygen and organic compounds. Notice that this process is the reverse of aerobic respiration, which changes oxygen and organic compounds into carbon dioxide and water. In other words, the products of photosynthesis are used in respiration, and the products of respiration are used in photosynthesis.

The organelle in plant cells that plays a vital role in photosynthesis is the chloroplast. Recall that chloroplasts are filled with a green pigment called chlorophyll. Chlorophyll and other pigments in the chloroplasts are grouped in clusters. These clusters of pigments trap light energy. In a complex series of reactions, this light energy is converted into chemical energy. This complex series consists of the light reactions of photosynthesis. The light reactions require light to operate. Photosynthesis also uses light energy to split water. Oxygen is produced when water is split.

The chemical energy produced in the light reaction is stored in two compounds—ATP and NADPH. Recall that respiration makes ATP to serve as the energy currency for cells. Photosynthesis makes ATP for another reason—to drive a second set of reactions. The second set of reactions in photosynthesis comprises the dark reactions, also known as the **Calvin cycle**. The Calvin cycle does not require light to operate. Instead, it depends on the ATP and NADPH made in the light reactions.

While ATP supplies the energy, NADPH supplies hydrogen atoms. These hydrogen atoms are used by the Calvin cycle to change carbon dioxide into organic compounds, primarily carbohydrates.

The overall equation for photosynthesis can be written as follows.

$$CO_2 + H_2O + \text{light energy} \rightarrow (CH_2O)_n + O_2$$

Recall that $(CH_2O)_n$ is the general formula for a carbohydrate where n represents the number of carbon atoms. A misconception about photosynthesis is that glucose is the main carbohydrate product. Actually, starch and sucrose (table sugar) are the main carbohydrate products of photosynthesis. Plant cells convert starch and sucrose to glucose for use in respiration. The fact that plant cells carry out respiration points to another misconception. Animal cells are not the only ones to carry out respiration. Plant cells also carry out respiration. However, plant cells carry out photosynthesis, something that animal cells cannot do.

UNIT 2

Review

Darken the circle by the best answer.

1. Which is the formula for a fat?
   - (A) CO_2
   - (B) C_6H_6
   - (C) $C_{51}H_{98}O_6$
   - (D) $C_{12}H_{22}O_{11}$

2. Identify the molecule that is always a product of dehydration synthesis.
   - (A) water
   - (B) a polypeptide
   - (C) glucose
   - (D) a saturated fat

3. An enzyme
   - (A) is saturated if it contains only single bonds.
   - (B) forms by joining fatty acids to make a larger molecule.
   - (C) is an example of a carbohydrate.
   - (D) consists of polypeptides.

4. How many ATP molecules are made from one glucose molecule under anaerobic conditions?
   - (A) 2
   - (B) 4
   - (C) 34
   - (D) 38

5. By accepting the hydrogen atoms that pass along the electron transport chain, oxygen turns into
   - (A) carbon dioxide.
   - (B) water.
   - (C) ATP.
   - (D) pyruvic acid.

6. Which is a product of photosynthesis that is used in respiration?
   - (A) carbon dioxide
   - (B) ATP
   - (C) NADPH
   - (D) oxygen

7. The oxygen produced in photosynthesis comes from
   - (A) glucose.
   - (B) carbon dioxide.
   - (C) water.
   - (D) light energy.

8. Explain what carbohydrates and lipids have in common. How are they different?

   _____

   _____

9. How can the equation for photosynthesis be changed so that it represents the equation for respiration?

   _____

UNIT 2  Organic Chemistry Word Search

The following puzzle contains terms related to carbohydrates, lipids, and proteins. Use the definitions or descriptions given below to find each term.

```
F H O P P H G U T Y D T D E Q F E A L U
E Q M U R W J M G R T I Y J W Q I K F E
E D I P I L A E P Q G E C K Q G O H M O
K V I Y G L S T A R C H R W F I W Z Z T
L Z A T T G E A E A O N A C T A S Z J C
Q O D N P L B B T R Y T C S K N X Y T O
Y G R E N E S O L U L L E C T U T C L S
M B O N N V P L Y L R R B I F U H E E Y
E H A I F Z S I J Q M A M I N O A C I D
R M S K S G Y S D B L E T E L O H Z B E
Z R X E R Q D M P K O A V E E K O L E E
C K O I M D H H E W M C S Z D G P Y U U
O M Y Y H Z T D I H S T R N N F Z K F C
L L W I S H R Y R E E V F W R M A D T K
M U J H Z B G C A R B O H Y D R A T E R
R Q R C V H T Z O X D K U H L A J L R T
L Y M T L D I L Y T Y E W U T J U T T W
E L L Q F G M O V O L E R H L W T T I O
U R S D R S Q P O M F M L O U K S S S V
I W Q Z I N T O X C J E G U I H Z P H L
```

1. the building block of a protein (9 letters)

2. a lipid found in cell membranes (11 letters)

3. a protein that speeds up a reaction rate (6 letters)

4. a molecule formed from polypeptides (7 letters)

5. a product of every dehydration synthesis (5 letters)

6. its general formula is $(CH_2O)_n$ (12 letters)

7. what two amino acids form when they join (9 letters)

8. the type of compound that contains much more carbon and hydrogen than oxygen (5 letters)

9. a fat that has only single bonds between its carbon atoms (12 letters)

10. the carbohydrate used to build cell walls (9 letters)

11. the capacity for doing work (6 letters)

12. the sum of all life processes (10 letters)

Unit 2, Energy and Life
Biology, SV 0423-9

UNIT 2

Organic Chemistry

> **Dehydration synthesis plays a role in the formation of carbohydrates, lipids, and proteins. Dehydration synthesis takes place by removing H from one molecule and by removing OH from a second molecule. The H and OH are then joined to form water, H_2O. For this reason, a dehydration synthesis reaction is also known as a condensation reaction.**

1. Draw the compound that forms by dehydration synthesis between the following two sugars.

2. Draw the compound that forms by dehydration synthesis between the following glycerol molecule and three fatty acids.

3. Draw the compound that forms by dehydration synthesis between the following two amino acids.

UNIT 2

Proteins

Proteins are made from 20 different amino acids. Every amino acid consists of a carbon atom. This carbon atom acts as the central point to which are attached three other atoms or groups of atoms. One is a hydrogen atom. The second is a NH_2 group of atoms. The third is a COOH group of atoms. The 20 amino acids differ from one another only in the fourth group that is attached to the central carbon atom. This fourth group is called the R group. For example, the simplest amino acid, glycine, has a hydrogen (H) atom as its R group. In contrast, alanine has the R group $-CH_3$ attached to the central carbon atom. Examine the following formulas for these and three other amino acids.

| glycine | alanine | serine | cysteine | phenylalanine |

Draw the polypeptide that consists of the following amino acid sequence.

serine — alanine — cysteine — glycine — phenylalanine

UNIT 2

Enzymes

Enzymes are essential for the functioning of any cell. A single organism may have thousands of different enzymes. Each enzyme is designed to speed up a particular chemical reaction. To function properly, enzymes must operate under certain conditions. For example, an enzyme functions best at a particular temperature. Examine the following graph which shows how two different enzymes, A and B, function at various temperatures. Then use the graph to answer the questions that follow.

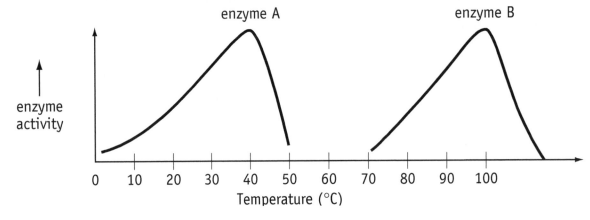

1. What is the optimal temperature for enzyme A? _____

2. What is the optimal temperature for enzyme B? _____

3. Which enzyme is likely to be found in an organism that lives in the boiling waters of a deep sea thermal vent? Explain the reason for your choice.

   _____

   _____

4. Which has the greater effect on enzyme activity—decreasing the temperature or increasing the temperature? Explain the reason for your choice. _____

   _____

   _____

UNIT 2

Respiration

> **The process of anaerobic respiration can be shown by the following chemical equations.**
>
> $$\text{lactic acid fermentation: } C_6H_{12}O_6 \rightarrow 2C_3H_6O_3 + 2ATP$$
>
> $$\text{alcoholic fermentation: } C_6H_{12}O_6 \rightarrow 2C_2H_5OH + 2CO_2 + 2ATP$$
>
> **The process of aerobic respiration can be shown by the following chemical equation.**
>
> $$C_6H_{12}O_6 + 6O_2 \rightarrow 6CO_2 + 6H_2O + energy$$

1. What is the chemical formula for lactic acid? _____

2. What is the chemical formula for ethyl alcohol? _____

3. Rewrite the equation for aerobic respiration so that it shows the energy produced in terms of

   ATP molecules. _____

> **Scientists have calculated that one glucose molecule releases 686 kilocalories of energy when it reacts completely with oxygen. Scientists have also calculated that 12 kilocalories of energy are required to make one ATP molecule. The efficiency of respiration can be calculated by using the following equation.**
>
> $$\text{efficiency of respiration} = \frac{\text{energy required to make ATP}}{\text{energy released by glucose}}$$

4. Calculate the efficiency of anaerobic respiration. Be sure to take into account the number of ATP molecules that are made.

5. Calculate the efficiency of aerobic respiration. Again be sure to take into account the number of ATP molecules that are made.

UNIT 2

Photosynthesis

Use the following list of words to complete the passage about photosynthesis. A word may be used more than once.

ATP	carbon dioxide	energy	NADPH
autotrophs	chemical	heterotrophs	oxygen
Calvin cycle	chloroplast	light	respiration
carbohydrates	dark reactions	light reactions	

As a result of photosynthesis, (1) _____ synthesize organic compounds that they use

as a source of (2) _____. Photosynthesis converts (3) _____ energy

into (4) _____ energy. Inside a (5) _____, chlorophyll pigments

absorb (6) _____ energy. This energy is then transferred to two chemical compounds—

(7) _____ and (8) _____. These compounds are made in a set of

reactions known as the (9) _____. These two compounds are then used to drive

another set of reactions known as the (10) _____ or (11) _____.

This second set of reactions changes (12) _____ into organic compounds known as

(13) _____. The (14)_____ that is produced in photosynthesis

comes from water molecules that are split by (15) _____ energy. As a result of

photosynthesis, (16) _____ and (17) _____ are changed into

(18) _____ and (19) _____. The products of photosynthesis are

used in another process called (20) _____. While photosynthesis is carried out only by

(21) _____, respiration is carried out by both (22) _____ and

(23) _____.

UNIT 2  Respiration and Photosynthesis

Determine whether the following features apply to respiration, photosynthesis, or both by placing an X in the appropriate column.

Feature	Respiration	Photosynthesis	Both
1. uses carbon dioxide	_____	_____	_____
2. uses oxygen	_____	_____	_____
3. produces ATP	_____	_____	_____
4. produces pyruvic acid	_____	_____	_____
5. depends on light energy	_____	_____	_____
6. involves the Krebs cycle	_____	_____	_____
7. involves the Calvin cycle	_____	_____	_____
8. occurs in autotrophs	_____	_____	_____
9. occurs in heterotrophs	_____	_____	_____
10. is part of metabolism	_____	_____	_____
11. can occur without oxygen	_____	_____	_____
12. produces carbohydrates	_____	_____	_____
13. requires pigment molecules	_____	_____	_____
14. forms water from oxygen	_____	_____	_____
15. forms oxygen from water	_____	_____	_____
16. includes dark reactions	_____	_____	_____
17. is more efficient with oxygen than without oxygen	_____	_____	_____
18. changes carbohydrates into carbon dioxide and water	_____	_____	_____
19. changes carbon dioxide and water into carbohydrates	_____	_____	_____

Part of the cell theory states that all cells come from preexisting cells. New cells arise by binary fission, mitosis, or meiosis. No matter what the process, the new cells receive chromosomes from the original cell. They may receive either a full set or half of what was present. If meiosis is involved, then the chromosomes may be transmitted from parents to offspring. Chromosomes contain the information that determines an individual's characteristics. The field of biology that focuses on how characteristics are transmitted from parents to offspring is called **genetics**. The first steps in understanding how genetics operate were taken by an Austrian monk named Gregor Mendel.

Mendelian Genetics

Mendel studied several characteristics or traits in garden peas. Working in the mid-1800s, Mendel carefully selected both the male and female plants and then grew the offspring in his garden. He began by using parent plants that were pure for each trait. These plants always produced offspring with the same

Key Terms

genetics—the field of biology that focuses on how characteristics are transmitted from parents to offspring

dominant—referring to a factor that masks another factor for the same trait

recessive—referring to a factor that is masked by another factor for the same trait

law of segregation—the segregation, or separation, of two factors for the same trait when a gamete forms

law of independent assortment—the independent segregation of the factors that control different traits

allele—an alternative form of a gene

Punnett square—a way to show the possible outcomes of a genetic cross

phenotype—the expression of the genotype of an organism

genotype—the genetic makeup of an organism

homozygous—the condition where both alleles of a pair are alike

heterozygous—the condition where both alleles of a pair are different

monohybrid cross—a cross between individuals that involves one trait

dihybrid cross—a cross between individuals that involves two traits

incomplete dominance—a situation where two or more alleles influence the phenotype, which is in between that of the parents

codominance—a situation where both alleles for a gene are expressed in a heterozygous individual

sex chromosome—a chromosome that carries the genes that determine an individual's sex

X-linked trait—a trait whose alleles are located only on the X chromosome

pedigree—a family history that shows individuals who display a particular trait and those who do not display the trait

trait. For example, plants pure for tall stems always produced offspring that grew to have tall stems.

Mendel called the parental generation the P generation. Offspring of the P generation make up the F_1 (first filial) generation. In turn, the offspring of the F_1 generation make up the F_2 (second filial) generation. In humans, the F_2 generation consists of the grandchildren, whose parents make up the F_1 generation, while the grandparents represent the P generation.

Mendel's experiments led to several conclusions. First, he concluded that each trait was controlled by two factors. One factor was **dominant** because it masked, or dominated, the other factor. The other factor was called the **recessive** factor. Second, Mendel concluded that the factors segregate, or separate, when a gamete forms. This became known as the **law of segregation.** Third, Mendel concluded that the factors for different characteristics are independently distributed to a gamete. This became known as the **law of independent assortment.**

Today, Mendel's factors are called **alleles.** An allele is defined as an alternative form of a gene. An allele is traditionally represented by a letter. A **Punnett square** is often used to show how traits are inherited. Consider a cross, or mating, between two rabbits. Both rabbits have black coat color, which is dominant to brown coat color. Therefore, B is used to represent black coat color. Brown coat color is represented by b. Assume that the alleles for coat color are different in both rabbits. Therefore, the genetic makeup for coat color in both rabbits is represented by Bb.

Coat color is known as the **phenotype**, which is the appearance of a trait in an organism. The letters Bb represent the **genotype**, which is the genetic makeup of an organism. Three genotypes are possible for coat color: BB, Bb, and bb. Both BB and bb are **homozygous** genotypes, where both alleles of a pair are alike. If the two alleles are different, such as Bb, then the organism is **heterozygous** for that trait. The following Punnett square illustrates the possible kinds of offspring that can be produced from a cross between two rabbits that are heterozygous for coat color. A cross between individuals that involves one trait, such as coat color, is called a **monohybrid cross.**

	B	b
B	BB	Bb
b	Bb	bb

The alleles contributed by one parent are placed along the top. The alleles contributed by the other parent are placed along the side. Each box represents a combination that is a possible genotype in the offspring. In this cross, the probabilities are 25% homozygous black individuals (BB), 50% heterozygous black individuals (Bb), and 25% homozygous brown individuals (bb).

Next, consider a cross between two pea plants heterozygous for two traits—seed shape and seed color. Round (R) is dominant to wrinkled (r). Yellow (Y) is dominant to green (y). The genotype for both parents is RrYy. The following Punnett square illustrates the possible combinations of genotypes in the F_1 generation. A cross between individuals that involves two traits, such as seed shape and seed color, is called a **dihybrid cross.**

	RY	Ry	rY	ry
RY	RRYY	RRYy	RrYY	RrYy
Ry	RRYy	RRyy	RrYy	Rryy
rY	RrYY	RrYy	rrYY	rrYy
ry	RrYy	Rryy	rrYy	rryy

Notice that four phenotypes are possible among the offspring: (1) round, yellow seeds; (2) round, green seeds; (3) wrinkled, yellow seeds, and (4) wrinkled, green seeds. Can you identify the nine genotypes that are responsible for these four phenotypes?

Unit 3, Genetics
Biology, SV 0423-9

Incomplete Dominance and Codominance

Genetics rarely operates as simply as Mendel thought. For example, Mendel's experiments led to the idea of dominant and recessive genes. However, offspring can sometimes have a phenotype in between that of the parents. This type of inheritance is called **incomplete dominance**. Consider what happens when a red-flowering four o'clock plant is crossed with a white-flowering four o'clock plant. All the offspring have pink flowers. Therefore, both alleles contribute to the phenotype, which is a pink color.

Notice what happens when two pink-flowering plants are crossed, as shown by the following Punnett square.

	R	W
R	RR	RW
W	RW	WW

Notice that in the case of incomplete dominance, neither allele may be assigned a capital letter to indicate which is dominant. In the case of the four o'clock plants, R represents the allele for red color, while W represents the allele for white color. In the cross shown above, the probable genotypic ratio is 1 RR : 2 RW : 1 WW. The probable phenotypic ratio is 1 red : 2 pink : 1 white.

Codominance occurs when both alleles for a gene are expressed in a heterozygous individual. In codominance, the alleles do not blend to produce the phenotype, as they do in incomplete dominance. Rather, both alleles are expressed. An example can be seen with coat color in horses. If a horse with red coat color is crossed with a horse with white coat color, then the offspring will have a roan coat color. The roan color is produced by the presence of both red hairs and white hairs on the horse. The following Punnett square illustrates codominance. Notice that the allele for red coat color is represented by R, while the allele for white coat color is represented by R'. A roan horse has the genotype RR'. What phenotypes do RR and R'R' represent?

	R	R
R'	RR'	RR'
R'	RR'	RR'

Blood Types

Mendel's experiments led him to conclude that a trait was controlled by two factors, or what are now called alleles. Today, scientists know that some traits are controlled by more than two alleles. In such cases, a trait is said to be controlled by multiple alleles. However, an individual can still possess only two alleles for that trait. An example of such a trait controlled by multiple alleles is human blood type.

Human blood types are controlled by three alleles—I^A, I^B, and i. Both I^A and I^B are dominant over i. However, I^A and I^B exhibit codominance. As a result, the six possible genotypes produce four phenotypes as shown in the following table.

Genotype	Phenotype (blood type)
$I^A I^A$ or $I^A i$	A
$I^B I^B$ or $I^B i$	B
$I^A I^B$	AB
ii	O

Assume that one parent is heterozygous for blood type A, and that the other parent is heterozygous for blood type B. The following Punnett square shows how these two parents can have children with all four blood types.

	I^A	i
I^B	$I^A I^B$	$I^B i$
i	$I^A i$	ii

Sex Linkage

Some traits are controlled by alleles located on the **sex chromosomes**. A sex chromosome carries the genes that determine an individual's sex. Sex chromosomes exist in two forms. One form is called the X chromosome. The other form is a shorter chromosome called the Y chromosome. In humans and many other organisms, the genes that cause an individual to be a male are located on the Y chromosome. Therefore, a person with a XX combination is a female, while a person with an XY combination is a male.

Traits whose alleles are located only on the X chromosome are said to be **X-linked traits**. An example of an X-linked trait in humans is hemophilia, a disease where the blood fails to clot. Hemophilia is caused by a recessive allele. Therefore, a female must have two recessive alleles to have hemophilia. The genotype of a female hemophiliac can be written as X^hX^h.

The genotype X^HX^H represents a normal female. The genotype X^HX^h is a normal female who is known as a carrier. Although she does not have hemophilia, she can pass the allele for the disease on to her children.

A male can have one of two genotypes, X^HY or X^hY. The X^HY genotype results in a normal male, while the X^hY results in a male hemophiliac. Notice that a male needs only one recessive allele to have hemophilia, while a female must have two recessive alleles.

Pedigrees

To analyze how traits are inherited, scientists sometimes construct a family history, or **pedigree**. By examining which relatives exhibit a trait, scientists can determine whether the gene is dominant or recessive and whether it is X-linked. For example, the following pedigree shows the presence of albinism in two generations. Albinism is a condition in which the body does not produce a pigment, causing the skin and hair to appear white.

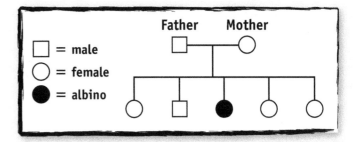

Notice that the parents have five children, four girls and one boy. Only one girl has albinism. This shows that albinism is controlled by a recessive allele. If albinism were caused by a dominant allele, then every individual with this condition would have a parent with albinism. Albinism is also not X-linked. If albinism were X-linked, then the father would also have the condition because he passes on his X chromosome to all his daughters, and not just one daughter.

UNIT 3

Review

Darken the circle by the best answer.

1. According to the law of independent assortment, which combination of alleles can be produced in a gamete of an individual that has the genotype AaBbcc?

   (A) Aa

   (B) AB

   (C) ABC

   (D) aBc

2. The phenotype of an organism is determined by its

   (A) F_2 cross.

   (B) genotype.

   (C) appearance.

   (D) Punnett square.

3. If both parents are heterozygous for two traits, then their genotype is

   (A) AaBb.

   (B) AaBB.

   (C) AABB.

   (D) aabb.

4. In codominance,

   (A) only one allele is expressed.

   (B) neither allele is expressed.

   (C) both alleles are expressed.

   (D) the offspring may show a phenotype in between that of the parents.

5. What genotype can a person with blood type B have?

   (A) ii

   (B) $I^A I^B$

   (C) I^B

   (D) $I^B i$

6. A pedigree helps a scientist determine

   (A) the cause of a disease.

   (B) how a trait is passed from one generation to the next.

   (C) which member of a family will definitely get a particular trait.

   (D) which chromosome carries the allele for a particular trait.

7. Explain why the results shown by a Punnett square are probable events and not certain events.

   _____

   _____

   _____

8. Why are X-linked conditions, such as hemophilia, much more common in males than in females?

   _____

   _____

   _____

UNIT 3

Genetics Puzzle

Use the clues to unscramble the letters to form a word. Then, unscramble all the circled letters to get the answer to the question

1. nege—the basic unit of heredity

__ __ ◯ __

2. lelale—what was once called a factor

__ __ ◯ __ __ __

3. digreepe—a family's genetic history

__ __ __ __ __ ◯ __ __

4. cistenge—the science of heredity

◯ __ __ ◯ __ __ __ __

5. nimandot—referring to a trait represented by an uppercase letter

◯ __ __ __ __ __ __ __

6. notpephey—the expression of the genotype of an organism

__ __ ◯ __ __ __ __ __ __

7. sorhomomec—where genes are found in the nucleus

__ __ ◯ __ __ __ __ __ ◯ __

8. hihepamoli—an X-linked disease

__ __ ◯ __ __ __ __ __ __ __

9. zoomushgoy—aa or BB but not Cc

__ __ __ ◯ __ __ ◯ __ __ __

Who started all this?

__ __ __ __ __ __ __ __   __ __ __ __ __ __

UNIT 3

Monohybrid Crosses

1. In rabbits, the allele for black coat color (B) is dominant over the allele for brown coat color (b). Use a Punnett square to predict the results of a cross between a rabbit heterozygous for black coat color and a rabbit that has brown coat color.

2. In pea plants, purple flower color (P) is dominant over white flower color (p). Use a Punnett square to predict the phenotypes and genotypes of a cross between pea plant homozygous for purple flower color and a pea plant homozygous for white flower color. If two plants from the F_1 generation are crossed, what genotypes and phenotypes are expected in the F_2 generation?

3. A testcross is sometimes done to determine the genotype of an individual that shows the dominant trait. For example, in guinea pigs black coat color (B) is dominant to brown coat color (b). A guinea pig with black coat color may be either homozygous dominant (BB) or heterozygous (Bb). In a testcross, the individual whose genotype is unknown is mated with an individual who shows the recessive trait and therefore must be homozygous recessive. For example, a guinea pig with brown coat color must have the genotype bb. Use Punnett squares to show what can happen when a guinea pig with brown coat color is crossed with two different guinea pigs, one homozygous for black coat color and the other heterozygous for black coat color. Explain why the appearance of a guinea pig with brown coat color in the F_1 generation proves that the guinea pig with black coat color in the P generation must be heterozygous.

UNIT 3

Dihybrid Crosses

1. In watermelons, the allele for solid green color (G) is dominant over the allele for striped pattern (g). Short shape (S) is dominant over long shape (s). A cross is made between a watermelon that is homozygous for green color and short shape and a watermelon that has a striped pattern and long shape. What is the genotype of each parent?

_____

2. Use a Punnett square to predict the phenotypes and genotypes of the F_1 generation produced by crossing the two watermelons described in question 1. Explain why it is possible for a dihybrid cross to produce only one phenotype in the offspring.

3. In guinea pigs, the allele for short hair (S) is dominant over the allele for long hair (s). The allele for black hair (B) is dominant over the allele for brown hair (b). What are the possible genotypes for a guinea pig that has short, black hair?

_____

4. A cross is made between two guinea pigs which are both heterozygous for short, black hair. Use a Punnett square to predict the genotypes and phenotypes in the F_1 generation.

5. What is the expected ratio of phenotypes in the F_1 generation in question 4? You should get the same ratio that Mendel obtained with his pea plants when he did a dihybrid cross between two plants heterozygous for both traits.

1. A cross between a snapdragon with red flowers and a snapdragon with white flowers produces plants that all have pink flowers. What are the genotypes for these three plants?

   _____

2. A snapdragon with red flowers is crossed with a snapdragon with pink flowers. Use a Punnett square to predict the genotypes and phenotypes of the F_1 generation.

3. A plant breeder wants to produce snapdragon plants that all have pink flowers. He decides that the best method is to cross only plants with pink flowers. Is his decision correct? Explain your answer with the help of a Punnett square.

   _____

4. In codominance, a horse with roan coat color inherits one allele, R, from one parent, and the other allele, R', from its other parent. Is it possible for one of its parents to have a roan coat color? Explain your answer.

   _____

   _____

5. Use a Punnett square to predict the offspring from a cross between two horses that both have roan coat color.

UNIT 3

Blood Types

1. A person can have one of four blood types— A, B, AB, and O. Explain why it is not possible for someone to have an ABO blood type.

_____

2. Use a Punnett square to show how it is possible for a father with blood type A and a mother with blood type B to have a child with blood type O.

3. Use a Punnett square to show why it is not possible for someone with blood type AB to be the child of a father with blood type O and a mother with blood type AB.

4. Use Punnett squares to show what blood types the children can have if the father has blood type B and the mother has blood type O.

5. What is the probability of a child having blood type A if the both the mother and father have blood type AB?

UNIT 3

Sex-Linkage

1. Explain why a father with an X-linked disease or disorder cannot pass this trait on to his sons.

_____

_____

2. Hemophilia is a recessive X-linked disease in humans. Use a Punnett square to predict the genotypes and phenotypes of children born to a father who is normal and a woman who is a carrier or heterozygous for this condition. Let X^H represent the normal allele and X^h represent the allele for hemophilia.

3. Colorblindness is another recessive X-linked disorder in humans. Many forms of colorblindness exist, but the most common is the inability to distinguish red from green. Use a Punnett square to predict the genotypes and phenotypes of children born to a father who has red-green colorblindness and a mother who is homozygous for normal vision. Let X^C represent the normal allele and X^c represent the allele for red-green colorblindness.

UNIT 3

Pedigrees

Examine the following pedigree which shows the inheritance of a genetic disorder in a family.

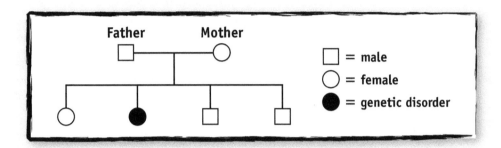

1. Is this genetic disorder inherited as a dominant or recessive trait? Explain your answer.

_____

_____

2. Is this genetic disorder inherited as an X-linked trait? Explain your answer.

_____

_____

3. Use a Punnett square to predict the genotypes and phenotypes of the children if the woman in the F_1 generation who has the disorder marries a male who does not carry an allele for this disorder.

Gregor Mendel discovered how certain traits are inherited. Based on his work, scientists discovered that genetics involves a variety of patterns of inheritance. They also discovered that traits were controlled by genes located on the chromosomes. The next steps were to determine the chemical nature of the gene and how a gene operates to express a particular trait. The answers are being found in a class of organic compounds known as **nucleic acids**. Nucleic acids are very large organic molecules that store information in the cell.

DNA

The nucleic acid that stores the genetic information as genes on a chromosome is **deoxyribonucleic acid**, DNA. DNA is a large molecule that consists of two chains twisted around each other. The building block that makes up each chain is called a nucleotide. A DNA nucleotide has three parts: (1) a sugar molecule called deoxyribose; (2) a phosphate group; and (3) a nitrogen-containing base. There are four nitrogen-containing bases in DNA: adenine (A), thymine (T), guanine (G), and cytosine (C).

In 1953, two scientists named James Watson and Francis Crick proposed a model as to how these four nucleotides were arranged to make up a DNA molecule. They suggested that DNA is composed of two nucleotide chains that wrap around each other to form a double spiral, like a spiral staircase. This structure is called a double helix, which is shown in the following illustration.

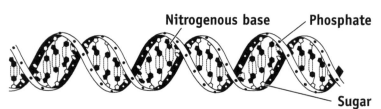

Nitrogenous base   **Phosphate**

Sugar

Double Helix

Key Terms

nucleic acid—a large organic molecule that stores and carries genetic information in the cell

deoxyribonucleic acid (DNA)—the nucleic acid that stores the genetic information as genes on a chromosome

replication—the process of copying DNA

ribonucleic acid—the molecule that is responsible for assembling proteins based on the genetic information contained in DNA

messenger RNA—the nucleic acid that carries the genetic information from the DNA in the nucleus to the cytoplasm

transfer RNA—the nucleic acid that transports amino acids to the ribosomes where they will be assembled into a protein

ribosomal RNA—the nucleic acid that combines with proteins to form the ribosomes

transcription—the process by which genetic information is copied from DNA to RNA

translation—the process of assembling amino acids based on the information in mRNA

codon—a sequence of three nitrogen-containing bases in mRNA that specifies a particular amino acid

anticodon—a sequence of three nitrogen-containing bases in tRNA that pairs with the three-base codon in mRNA

Notice that the sugars and phosphate groups form the "backbone" of the molecule. The four bases form the "steps" of the double helix. The bases always form pairs. These pairs of bases are called complementary base pairs. There are two complementary base pairs: A — T and G — C.

Each base pair is held together by a relatively weak bond. These bonds are broken when a cell is about to undergo mitosis. Each chromosome must be duplicated before mitosis starts so that each cell receives the proper genetic information. The duplication of a chromosome means that the DNA must be copied. The process of copying DNA is called **replication**.

Replication begins with the breaking of bonds between the base pairs. This happens simultaneously at different sites along a chromosome. The breaking of these bonds separates the two chains of the double helix. Nucleotides in the nucleus are then joined to the nucleotides on each chain. This process is always done according to complementary base pairing. Therefore, if A is present on a chain, then only T can be paired with it. Likewise, if C is present on a chain, then only G can be paired with it. As a result of replication, two DNA molecules are produced, each identical to the original. The following diagram illustrates the process of replication.

RNA

DNA directs the synthesis of proteins. However, DNA is found mainly in the nucleus of a cell while protein synthesis occurs in the cytoplasm. How then does a molecule in the nucleus control a process that occurs in the cytoplasm? The answer can be found in the second type of nucleic acid—**ribonucleic acid**, RNA. RNA is the molecule that is responsible for assembling proteins based on the genetic information contained in DNA.

Three major differences in structure exist between DNA and RNA. First, RNA contains the sugar ribose, whereas DNA contains the sugar deoxyribose. Second, RNA contains the base uracil (U) in place of thymine (T). Third, RNA exists in three different types. Each type plays a different role in protein synthesis.

One type of RNA is called **messenger RNA** (mRNA). Messenger RNA carries the genetic information from the DNA in the nucleus to the cytoplasm. A second type of RNA is called **transfer RNA** (tRNA), which transports amino acids to the ribosomes where they will be assembled into a protein. A third type of RNA is called **ribosomal RNA** (rRNA), which combines with proteins to form the ribosomes.

All RNA molecules are made from DNA in a process called **transcription**. During transcription, the two strands of a DNA molecule separate just as they do in replication. However, enzymes involved in transcription will direct the synthesis of RNA from one of the DNA strands. Base pairings are also followed in transcription, just as they are in replication. However, in transcription, uracil (U) pairs with adenine (A). The following figure illustrates the process of transcription.

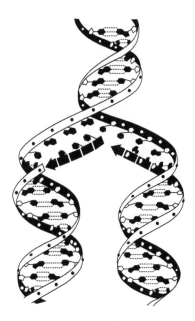

Replication

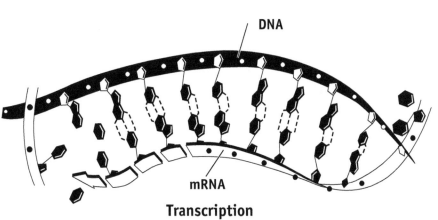

DNA

mRNA

Transcription

Protein Synthesis

A sequence of nitrogen-containing bases in DNA will direct the order in which amino acids are assembled into a protein. This process begins with transcription. The mRNA that is made by transcription moves from the nucleus to the cytoplasm where it attaches to ribosomes. Here is where the amino acids will be assembled. The process of assembling amino acids based on the information in mRNA is called **translation**.

Recall that tRNA transfers amino acids floating freely in the cytoplasm to the ribosomes. The genetic information in mRNA is decoded in a series of three nitrogen-containing bases. Each combination of three such bases in mRNA is called a **codon**. Each codon codes for a specific amino acid.

A three-base combination is also found on tRNA. The sequence of three nitrogen-containing bases on tRNA is called an **anticodon**. The tRNA anticodon is complementary to and pairs with its corresponding mRNA codon.

For example, assume that mRNA contains the codon UUU. A tRNA with the anticodon AAA would pair with this mRNA codon. A tRNA with the anticodon AAA is specific for the amino acid phenylalanine. Assume that the next mRNA codon is GGG. A tRNA with the anticodon CCC would pair with this mRNA codon. A tRNA with the anticodon CCC is specific for the amino acid glycine. This glycine molecule is then joined to the phenylalanine molecule. Therefore, the two mRNA codons have specified the amino acid sequence: phenylalanine-glycine.

Translation continues until all the amino acids have been assembled into a polypeptide. The polypeptide is released from the ribosome. It then may combine with other polypeptides and fold to form a functional protein. The following diagram illustrates the process of translation.

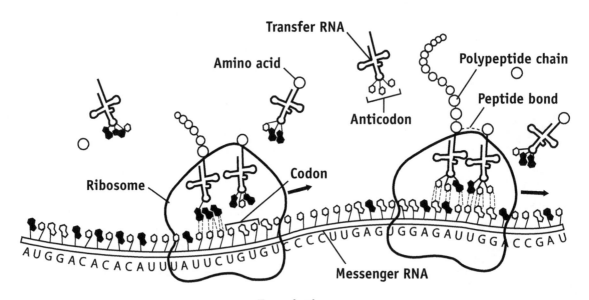

Translation

UNIT 4

Review

Darken the circle by the best answer.

1. Which represents a correct base pair found in a DNA molecule?

   (A) G—A

   (B) C—T

   (C) C—G

   (D) T—U

2. DNA replication involves the

   (A) synthesis of proteins.

   (B) formation of messenger RNA.

   (C) separation of the two strands that make up the double helix.

   (D) substitution of the nitrogen-containing base T in place of G.

3. Unlike DNA, RNA

   (A) is a large molecule made up of nucleotides.

   (B) contains the sugar ribose.

   (C) is found mainly in the nucleus of a cell.

   (D) contains the nitrogen-containing base thymine.

4. In transcription,

   (A) RNA is synthesized from DNA.

   (B) DNA is synthesized from RNA.

   (C) a protein is made on the ribosomes.

   (D) an exact copy of a DNA molecule is made in the nucleus.

5. In translation, what anticodon on tRNA pairs with the mRNA codon AUC?

   (A) AUC

   (B) TAG

   (C) UAG

   (D) UUU

6. Amino acids are assembled into a specific order

   (A) on the ribosomes.

   (B) according to a sequence of nitrogen-containing bases.

   (C) depending on codon-anticodon pairings.

   (D) all of the above

7. Describe what is meant by a double helix.

   _____

   _____

   _____

   _____

   _____

8. What is the role of ribosomes in protein synthesis?

   _____

   _____

   _____

   _____

   _____

UNIT 4

DNA and Replication

1. Why is the structure of a DNA molecule sometimes referred to as having the shape of a spiral staircase?

_____

_____

2. What nitrogen-containing base pairs are found in a DNA molecule?

_____

3. Explain why DNA replication must occur before mitosis starts.

_____

_____

Examine the following illustration which shows a short piece of a DNA molecule.

4. Fill in the letter for each missing nitrogen-containing base.

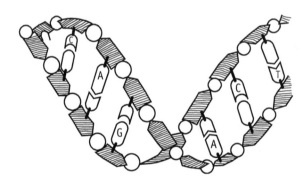

5. Draw the DNA molecules that form after the piece of DNA shown above replicates. How do these molecules compare to the original molecule?

UNIT 4  RNA and Transcription

Use the following list of words to complete the passage below concerning the structure and function of RNA. There is one word on the list that you will not use.

adenine	double helix	phosphate	thymine
complementary	guanine	ribose	transcription
cytoplasm	messenger RNA	ribosomes	transfer RNA
cytosine	nucleus	ribosomal RNA	uracil
deoxyribose			

RNA is different from DNA in several ways. Whereas DNA contains the sugar (1) _____,

RNA contains the sugar (2) _____. In addition, RNA is made using the

nitrogen-containing base (3) _____, while DNA contains the base

(4) _____. Both RNA and DNA, however, contain (5) _____

groups. Unlike DNA, RNA exists in three different types. One type, known as (6) _____,

carries the genetic information from the (7) _____ to the (8) _____

where the proteins are synthesized. A second type of RNA, called (9) _____,

transports the amino acids to the (10) _____. These structures are made of proteins.

The third type of RNA is called (11) _____. All three types of RNA are made from

DNA in a process called (12) _____. Just as the DNA does in replication, the two

strands of the (13) _____ separate. Then DNA makes a strand of RNA that is

(14) _____ to the base sequence of the DNA. Therefore, the nitrogen-containing base

(15) _____ will pair with a cytosine base in DNA, while (16) _____

will pair with a thymine base in DNA.

What is the only word that you did not use from the list above to complete this passage?

(17) _____

UNIT 4  Protein Synthesis

There are 64 possible codons. There are only 20 amino acids that make up proteins. Therefore, more than one codon specifies the same amino acid. For example, the codons GUU, GUC, GUA, and GUG specify the amino acid valine. One codon is responsible for starting translation. This start codon is AUG. Several codons stop translation. As a result, all 64 codons are accounted for in one way or another. The following table lists all 64 codons and the amino acid each codon specifies.

UUU UUC } Phenylalnine UUA UUG } Leucine	UCU UCC UCA UCG } Serine	UAU UAC } Tyrosine UAA UAG } Stop	UGU UGC } Cysteine UGA } Stop UGG } Tryptophan
CUU CUC CUA CUG } Leucine	CCU CCC CCA CCG } Proline	CAU CAC } Histidine CAA CAG } Glutamine	CGU CGC CGA CGG } Arginine
AUU AUC AUA } Isoleucine AUG } Start	ACU ACC ACA ACG } Threonine	AAU AAC } Asparagine AAA AAG } Lysine	AGU AGC } Serine AGA AGG } Arginine
GUU GUC GUA GUG } Valine	GCU GCC GCA GCG } Alanine	GAU GAC } Aspartic acid GAA GAG } Glutamic acid	GGU GGC GGA GGG } Glycine

Assume that you have the following sequence of nitrogen-containing bases in DNA:

G—G—C—C—T—A—C—A—T—G—G—C—C—A—A—A—G—G—T—C—A—C—T—T—A—A—T—T—C

1. Transcribe the sequence above into mRNA.

_____

2. Use the table above to translate the mRNA into a sequence of amino acids. Be sure to look for both start and stop codons.

_____

UNIT 4  Genetic Engineering

> *A new class of enzymes was discovered in the late 1960s. These enzymes cut through the two strands of a DNA molecule in such a way that each strand is left with several unpaired nitrogen-containing bases. Such DNA fragments can then be joined and sealed to form an intact molecule. In effect, a new DNA molecule can be designed and constructed. This process is known as genetic engineering. Genetic engineering involves inserting segments of DNA taken from one organism into the DNA of another organism.*

1. A species is defined as a group of organisms that can mate and produce fertile offspring in nature. Consider that genetic engineering has taken human genes and inserted them into bacterial DNA molecules. Explain why this product of genetic engineering is called recombinant DNA.

_____

_____

2. Bacteria divide very rapidly so that multiple copies of the human gene are produced in a very short time. Hopefully, the human genes will be active and produce proteins. These proteins can then be isolated and harvested. For example, genetic engineering is used to enable bacteria to produce a human growth hormone. How does this demonstrate that genetic engineering can benefit humans?

_____

_____

3. Consider a plant species that is resistant to certain pests. This resistance is due to a gene for pest resistance. Describe how genetic engineering can be used to make another plant species resistant to these pests.

_____

_____

Every year, thousands of new kinds of organisms are discovered. Scientists are not sure how many more new kinds of organisms remain to be discovered. They are not even sure how many different kinds of organisms inhabit the Earth. What scientists do know, however, is that the number of different kinds of organisms on Earth is extremely large. At least 10 million and perhaps as many as 200 million different kinds of organisms exist. This is really not surprising when you consider how old Earth is.

Earth's History

Based on experimental data, scientists think that Earth developed as a planet some 4.6 billion years ago. The oldest rocks on Earth date from about 4.2 billion years ago. This finding suggests that it took 400 million years for Earth to cool to a temperature below the melting point of rock. During this time, Earth also grew increasingly larger as it was bombarded with debris from space.

Conditions that are found in volcanoes today are thought to be similar to conditions present on Earth 4.2 billion years ago. Temperatures were extremely high. Atmospheric conditions were violent. Gases spewed into the atmosphere as volcanoes erupted continually.

Based on the contents of volcanic gases, scientists think that Earth's primitive atmosphere contained ammonia, hydrogen gas, water vapor, and methane gas. Scientists have subjected these gases to conditions thought to have been present on the primitive Earth. These experiments show that simple organic compounds can form from these gases under those conditions. Scientists have also shown that these simple organic compounds can arrange themselves into droplets.

The first life forms are thought to have developed on Earth some 3.5 billion years ago. This date was established when scientists discovered the oldest-known **fossil** of an organism.

Key Terms

fossil—a trace of a long-dead organism

homologous structure—a structure that has a different function in various organisms but shares a common ancestry

vestigial structure—a structure present in an organism that has no function

embryo—a fertilized egg cell that has started to divide and grow

macromolecule—a very large molecule, such as a protein or nucleic acid

natural selection—the theory that organisms best suited to their environment reproduce more successfully than others

adaptation—a trait or behavior that increases an organism's chances of survival

species—a group of organisms that can mate with one another and produce fertile offspring

This discovery was made in Australia. This organism was a prokaryote, the simplest form of life. Scientists think that these first prokaryotes were heterotrophs, which took in organic molecules from their environment. For about 2 billion years, heterotrophic prokaryotes were the only living things on Earth. Autotrophs and eukaryotes came later, making their appearance between 2 and 1.5 billion years ago. From this point in time, life began to evolve until it reached the huge diversity that it now displays.

Evolution: Facts

Scientists have uncovered evidence supporting the fact that evolution has occurred over Earth's long history. Evolution simply means that life forms have changed over time. Organisms have appeared and survived on Earth for long periods of time. Many changed while they lived. Many became extinct. New types of organisms took their place.

A major piece of evidence in support of evolution is the fossil record. A fossil is a trace of a long-dead organism. In 1668, Robert Hooke first suggested that fossils are the remains of plants and animals. Today, scientists know that fossils are formed in various ways. They also know that the fossil record is incomplete because most organisms that lived in the past never left a fossil record. Conditions must be just right for an organism to become a fossil. One requirement is that a dead organism is quickly buried by dust, sand, or mud deposited by wind or water. Hard body parts also favor fossil formation.

The fossil record has provided a picture of how certain animals have evolved. For example, fossils show that modern whales have evolved from

four-legged animals that lived on land. These land animals also gave rise to horses and cows. Fossils of various animals show this evolutionary history that took place over some 60 million years.

Another piece of evidence in support of evolution is the presence of **homologous structures**. A homologous structure is a structure that has a different function in different organisms but shares a common ancestry. For example, a bird's wing, a dolphin's fin, and a person's arm are homologous structures. Each has a different function. However, all three structures have bones in the same position and order. This observation points to the evolution of these structures from a common ancestor.

Another line of evidence in support of evolution comes from **vestigial structures**. A vestigial structure is a structure present in an organism that has no obvious function. For example, whales have a pelvis. In humans and other animals, a pelvis serves as the point of attachment for the leg bones used for movement. Whales obviously have no need for leg bones or a pelvis because they use their powerful tails to swim. In addition to the fossil record, the whale's pelvis is evidence of its evolution from a four-legged land animal.

Still another line of evidence in support of evolution comes from the stages of **embryo** development. An embryo is a fertilized egg cell that has started to divide and grow. Although the adult organisms look quite different, the early stages of development of fish, rabbit, and gorilla embryos look remarkably similar. This observation suggests that these organisms share a common ancestor from which they have evolved.

A final line of evidence in support of evolution comes from a study of **macromolecules** in organisms. A macromolecule is a very large molecule, such as a protein or nucleic acid. For example, the protein hemoglobin in humans and gorillas differ by only one amino acid. The genetic code in both organisms is identical. The codon UUU, for example, specifies the amino acid phenylalanine in both humans and gorillas. In fact, the genetic code in DNA is the same for almost all organisms. The universality of the genetic code points to an evolutionary relationship between all organisms.

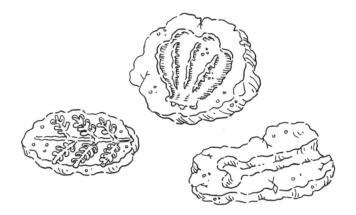

Unit 5, Biological Diversity
Biology, SV 0423-9

Evolution: Theory

In 1859, Charles Darwin published a book titled *On the Origin of Species by Means of Natural Selection*, commonly known as *The Origin of Species*. In his book, Darwin proposed a theory about how evolution occurred. At this time, many scientists accepted the evidence supporting evolution. However, they did not know how evolution took place. Darwin proposed that evolution occurred by a process he called **natural selection**. The theory of natural selection states that organisms best suited to their environment reproduce more successfully than others. Therefore, the proportion of organisms with these traits increases over generations. In contrast, organisms that lack these traits produce fewer offspring. Over generations, the proportion of these organisms decreases.

The key to Darwin's theory is a trait that is best suited to the environment. Such a trait is called an **adaptation**. An example of how natural selection operates can be seen in giraffes that evolved to have very long necks. Natural selection states that giraffes that have necks long enough to reach higher for food are best suited to their environment. Therefore, a long neck is an adaptation. As food gets higher to reach, only giraffes with long enough necks can survive and reproduce. Over generations, this leads to the evolution of giraffes with very long necks.

Although Darwin developed the theory of natural selection, he could not explain how evolution occurred in terms of genetics. At the time, nothing was known about genetics and how traits were inherited. Since Darwin's time, scientists have updated Darwin's theory to explain it in terms of genetics. They also can explain how organisms can change so much over time that a new **species** forms. A species consists of organisms that can mate with one another and produce fertile offspring. When the individuals of two populations can no longer interbreed, the two populations are considered different species. Over Earth's long history, many millions of new species have evolved.

Classification

Evolution has led to the development of millions of different species. Even before Darwin's time, one goal of scientists was to organize the many different kinds of organisms into a system that made it easier to study them. In the 1750s, a Swedish scientist named Carl Linnaeus developed such a system. He published several books cataloging thousands of organisms. Linnaeus gave each species a two-word Latin name. For example, all humans were given the name *Homo sapiens*.

Two different organisms cannot be given the same scientific name. They may share one name but not both names. For example, two different types of oak trees have the names *Quercus rubra* and *Quercus phellos*. The second name can also be the same. A lizard has the name *Anolis carolinensis*, while a chickadee has the name *Parus carolinensis*.

The second name represents an organism's species. The first name represents its genus. A genus is more inclusive than a species. Linnaeus classified organisms into a system or groups that increase in inclusiveness. Since Linnaeus's time, scientists have increased the number of groups that make up the classification hierarchy. From least inclusive to most inclusive, these groups include species, genus, family, order, class, phylum, and kingdom.

Species with similar characteristics are grouped into the same genus. Genera with similar characteristics are grouped into the same family, and so on. There are six kingdoms: Archaebacteria, Eubacteria, Protista, Fungi, Plantae, and Animalia. All members of the kingdom Animalia are multicellular, eukaryotic, heterotrophic organisms. In contrast, all members of the kingdom Plantae are multicellular, eukaryotic, autotrophic organisms.

Since Linnaeus's time, about 1.5 million species have been identified and named. Scientists estimate that at least 8.5 million remain to be identified and named. Many of these live in the tropics, especially in the rain forests. The destruction of the rain forests has wiped out many of these species before scientists had a chance to identify them. No one knows how many of these species may have been valuable to humans as a source of food or medicine.

UNIT 5

Review

Darken the circle by the best answer.

1. How long ago do scientists think the Earth was formed?

   Ⓐ 1.5 billion years

   Ⓑ 2 billion years

   Ⓒ 4.2 billion years

   Ⓓ 4.6 billion years

2. The first organism to appear on Earth was a(n)

   Ⓐ autotroph.

   Ⓑ heterotroph.

   Ⓒ eukaryotic cell.

   Ⓓ plant cell.

3. Homologous structures have

   Ⓐ similar structures but different functions.

   Ⓑ similar functions but different structures.

   Ⓒ no known function.

   Ⓓ no fossil record.

4. The theory of natural selection states that

   Ⓐ all organisms are well-suited to their environment.

   Ⓑ all organisms have an equal chance of survival.

   Ⓒ adaptations are important to evolution.

   Ⓓ evolution occurs only in animals.

5. Which classification level is the most inclusive?

   Ⓐ genus

   Ⓑ order

   Ⓒ class

   Ⓓ family

6. If two different organisms are classified in the same order, they can belong to different

   Ⓐ classes.

   Ⓑ phyla.

   Ⓒ kingdoms.

   Ⓓ families.

7. Name three types of evidence that support the occurrence of evolution.

   _____

   _____

   _____

   _____

   _____

8. Explain the role that adaptation plays in natural selection.

   _____

   _____

   _____

   _____

   _____

UNIT 5  Earth's History

Use the following table to answer the questions concerning the history of life on Earth.

End date (millions of years ago)	Era	Period	Epoch	Organisms
	Cenozoic	Quarternary	Recent	modern humans arise
0.1			Pleistocene	humans arise
2		Tertiary	Pliocene	large carnivores arise
5			Miocene	mammals diversify
24			Oligocene	diverse grazing animals arise
37			Eocene	early horses arise
58			Paleocene	more modern mammals arise
67	Mesozoic	Cretaceous		dinosaurs go extinct; mass extinction
144		Jurassic		dinosaurs diversify; birds arise
208		Triasic		primitive mammals arise; mass extinction; dinosaurs arise
245	Paleozoic	Permian		seed plants arise; reptiles diversify; mass extinction
286		Carboniferous		reptiles arise
360		Devonian		amphibians arise; mass extinction
408		Silurian		land plants arise
438		Ordovician		fishes arise; mass extinction
505		Cambrian		marine invertebrates arise
550	Precambrian			prokaryotes, then eukaryotes arise

1. How long ago did dinosaurs first appear on Earth? _____

2. How long did dinosaurs live on Earth? _____

3. Why was a popular movie named *Jurassic Park*?

_____

4. During what period did cows and sheep arise? _____

Earth's History (cont'd.)

5. How long did it take for seed plants to evolve after plants had the adaptations to survive on land?

_____

_____

6. What do the Cretaceous and Ordovician periods have in common?

_____

_____

7. In what era did the first organisms arise? _____

8. Which epoch lasted longer—the Miocene or the Eocene?

_____

9. In which period did frogs and salamanders arise?

_____

10. In which period did alligators and crocodiles arise?

_____

UNIT 5  Evolution: Facts and Theory

Determine whether each of the following statements is true or false by circling the appropriate letter. If the statement is false, rewrite it so that it is true.

1. A homologous structure serves no function.   T or F

_____

2. A study of macromolecules can provide evidence of evolution.   T or F

_____

3. Natural selection states that all organisms have the adaptations to survive in their environment.   T or F

_____

4. Those organisms that are adapted to survive are less likely to interbreed and produce offspring.   T or F

_____

5. Similarities between the early stages of embryo development of two different organisms are an indication that they will look very similar as adults.   T or F

_____

6. The term "survival of the fittest" is often associated with the theory of natural selection. The term "survival of the fittest" refers to the survival of the strongest organisms in a population.   T or F

_____

7. A small percentage of sperm whales possess tiny leg bones. These leg bones are an example of a vestigial structure.   T or F

_____

8. The scientific explanation as to how evolution occurs is accepted as fact.   T or F

_____

9. The evolution of living things is supported by several sources of evidence.   T or F

_____

UNIT 5    Classification I

Collect ten small objects you have in your house. Buttons of different sizes, colors, shape, etc., would be ideal. You can also use items such as a paper clip, a refrigerator magnet, a bottle cap, a small fork, a ruler, a pencil, a thumb tack, a coin, a straw, and an eraser. Think of a way to classify these objects. You can start by dividing your objects into two or three groups. For example, if you are using buttons, use size to start your classification system. You may divide the buttons into three groups: large, medium, and small. If you are using something other than buttons, you can start by classifying your objects based on their use.

When you have finished developing your classification system, each object should be in a category by itself. Once an item is in a category by itself, you have finished classifying that object. Use the space below to show how your classification system was developed. For example, you might start as follows.

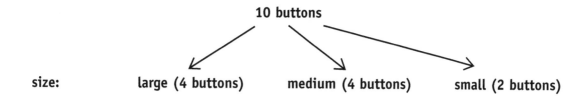

UNIT 5  Classification: Dichotomous Keys

> *Trying to identify an organism can be a difficult task. You could try to compare the organism to those described in a classification system. However, this process can very time consuming. People often use a dichotomous key to identify an organism or other object such as a mineral. A dichotomous key uses pairs of contrasting descriptive statements to lead to the identification of an organism.*

Use the dichotomous key provided to identify the six leaves below. Begin with paired descriptions 1a and 1b and follow the instructions. Proceed through the key until you have identified each leaf.

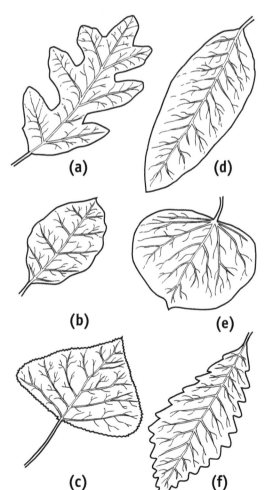

(a) (d)

(b) (e)

(c) (f)

Dichotomous Key for Identifying Common Leaves

1a. If the edge of the leaf has no teeth, or lobes, go to 2 in the key.

1b. If the edge of the leaf has teeth, or lobes, go to 3 in the key.

2a. If the leaf has slightly wavy edges, it is a shingle oak.

2b. If the leaf has smooth edges, go to 4 in the key.

3a. If the leaf edge is toothed, it is a Lombardy poplar.

3b. If the leaf edge has lobes, go to 5 in the key.

4a. If the leaf is heart-shaped with veins branching from the base, it is a redbud.

4b. If the leaf is not heart-shaped, it is a live oak.

5a. If the leaf edge has a few large lobes, it is an English oak.

5b. If the leaf edge has many small lobes, it is a chestnut oak.

(a) _____

(b) _____

(c) _____

(d) _____

(e) _____

(f) _____

UNIT 5 Biological Diversity Crossword

Across

3. type of structure that has no function

6. kingdom that includes you

8. what teachers like to have in class or what several families make up in the classification system

9. change in organisms over time

11. what *Homo* represents in *Homo sapiens*

12. trait that evolved in giraffes

14. unit in school or what orders make up

15. what an organism needs to survive

17. structures that have different functions but share a common ancestry

20. early stage of development

22. type of organism that was first to evolve

23. type of organism that evolved later

24. kingdom to which an oak tree belongs

Down

1. what an organism may become after it dies

2. what you find in a home or what several genera make up in the classification system

4. organisms that diversified during the Jurassic period

5. what members of the same species can do

7. Darwin's theory of evolution

10. developed the modern classification system

13. most inclusive classification category

16. not a fact but an explanation that has been tested many times

18. gas thought to have been present in Earth's primitive atmosphere

19. group of organisms that can interbreed successfully

21. another gas thought to have been present in Earth's atmosphere

Unit 5, Biological Diversity
Biology, SV 0423-9

Organisms are continually interacting with their environment. They interact with other living things and with nonliving components of their environment such as water and sunlight. Studying these interactions is important to understanding how organisms are able to survive and maintain their species. Such knowledge can also be useful in preventing a species from becoming extinct. The study of the interactions between organisms and their environment is called **ecology**. Ecology involves collecting information about organisms and their environment, looking for patterns, and seeking to explain these observations and patterns.

From Biosphere to Biomes

Various levels of organization exist throughout biology. For example, each organism is classified into seven levels of categories: species, genus, family, order, class, phylum, and kingdom. A level of organization also exists in ecology. The most inclusive level is the **biosphere**, which is the portion of Earth and its atmosphere that support life. The biosphere is composed of smaller units called **ecosystems**. An ecosystem includes all the organisms and the nonliving environment found in a particular place. For example, a pond is an example of an ecosystem.

Key Terms

ecology—the study of the interactions between organisms and their environment, which includes both living and nonliving components

biosphere—the area on and around Earth where life exists

ecosystem—all the organisms and the nonliving environment found in a particular place

community—all the living things in an ecosystem

population—all the members of a species that live in the same area

biome—a geographic land area characterized by particular types of animals and plants

producer—an autotrophic organism that captures energy to make organic molecules

food chain—the pathway through which energy flows in an ecosystem

consumer—a heterotroph that obtains energy by feeding upon other organisms or organic waste materials

herbivore—a consumer that eats a producer

carnivore—a consumer that eats other consumers

omnivore—a consumer that is both an herbivore and a carnivore

decomposer—an organism that breaks down wastes and complex molecules in dead organisms into simpler molecules

food web—the interconnected food chains in an ecosystem

transpiration—the process by which plants release water into the atmosphere

global warming—the increase in Earth's average temperature caused by "greenhouse" gases

Food Chains and Food Webs

No matter what biome they inhabit, all organisms must obtain energy to survive. Autotrophs capture energy that they transfer to organic molecules. Plants do this through photosynthesis. Autotrophs are known as **producers**. Most producers are photosynthetic. Plants are the major producers in all biomes. The most productive biome is a tropical rain forest. Although they occupy only 5 percent of Earth's surface, tropical rain forests account for almost 30 percent of the world's productivity.

The pathway through which energy flows in an ecosystem is called a **food chain**. An example of a food chain would be grass seeds → mouse → snake → hawk. In this food chain, the grass is the producer. The mouse, snake, and hawk are known as **consumers**, which are organisms that eat other organisms or organic waste materials. Consumers can be grouped according to the food they eat. **Herbivores** eat producers. **Carnivores** eat other consumers. Therefore, the mouse is an herbivore, while the snake and hawk are carnivores. An organism that is both an herbivore and a carnivore is called an **omnivore.**

Only about 10 percent of the total energy available at one level in a food chain is transferred to the next level. The rest of this energy—about 90 percent—is used by the organisms to survive and reproduce. The more energy an organism uses, the less will be available to transfer to the next level in the food chain. In addition, some of the organisms at one level in a food chain escape being eaten. When these organisms die, they become food for **decomposers**. A decomposer is an organism that breaks down wastes and complex molecules in dead organisms into simpler molecules. These simpler molecules are then returned to the soil or water.

As a result of the limited flow of energy through a food chain, each level can support only a much smaller number of organisms at the next level. The top level of a food chain is always much smaller in number than the lower levels. For this reason, the feeding relationships in a food chain are sometimes referred to as a food pyramid.

Because only about 10 percent of the energy is transferred from one level to the next level, there is

All the living things in an ecosystem make up a **community**. In turn, a community is made up of **populations**. Each population includes all the members of a species that live in one place at the same time. For example, in a pond ecosystem, the community consists of all the living things including fishes, turtles, insects, and aquatic plants. Even a simple community may contain thousands of species. Each species within the community represents a population. For example, all the rainbow trout *Oncorhynchus mykiss* make up one population in the community that is part of a pond ecosystem.

The various ecosystems found in a particular geographic area make up a level of organization known as a biome. A **biome** is distinguished by the presence of characteristic plants and animals. However, a biome is commonly identified by its dominant plant life. For example, evergreen trees, such as pines and firs, characterize a biome called a taiga. Like all biomes, a taiga can be found in more than one place on Earth.

Biomes seldom have distinct boundaries. Rather, one biome gradually changes into another biome. This gradual change from one biome to another is the result of the gradual change in climate over Earth's surface. Nonetheless, Earth's land surface can be divided into seven major biomes: tundra, taiga, temperate deciduous forest, temperate grassland, desert, savanna, and tropical rain forest. Antarctica is the only land surface on Earth that has no biome.

not enough energy at the higher levels to support additional levels. For this reasons, food chains are usually short, consisting of between three and five types of organisms.

The feeding relationships within an ecosystem are usually too complex to be represented by a single food chain. Instead, many consumers eat more than one type of food. In addition, one type of organism may serve as food for several other types of organisms. As a result, several food chains may actually be linked to form a more complex picture of the feeding relationships within an ecosystem. This more complex picture is called a **food web**. A food web provides a more detailed picture of how organisms interact for food within an ecosystem.

Cycles in Ecosystems

The arrows in a food chain and a food web indicate that energy flows in only one direction. In contrast, water and other substances are recycled and reused. If these substances were not recycled, the effect on ecosystems would be disastrous. The recycling of water is a perfect example. The availability of water is one of the key factors that influence the productivity of an ecosystem. The less water that is available, the less organic material that can be made by the autotrophs.

Water is found on Earth in bodies of water such as lakes, rivers, streams, and the oceans. In addition, water is found in the atmosphere in the form of water vapor. Water is also present in the ground, either in soil or porous rock deeper under the surface. The movement of water between the atmosphere, the ground, and bodies of water is known as the water cycle.

Three processes make up the water cycle. The first process is precipitation. Precipitation cycles water from the atmosphere back to Earth in the form of rain, snow, sleet, hail, and fog. The second process is evaporation, which cycles water from Earth back to the atmosphere. The third process involved in the water cycle is **transpiration**. Transpiration is the release of water by plants. Transpiration is responsible for returning at least 90 percent of the water from land back to the atmosphere.

Another cycle found in ecosystems is the carbon cycle, which involves four processes. One process is respiration, which releases carbon dioxide into the atmosphere. Another process that releases carbon dioxide into the atmosphere is combustion. A third process, decomposition, also releases carbon dioxide into the atmosphere. This process is carried out by decomposers that break down organic compounds in dead organisms and waste products.

The fourth process is the only one that removes carbon dioxide from the atmosphere. This process is photosynthesis. Until recently, the carbon cycle has been operating to keep the amount of carbon dioxide in balance between the atmosphere and Earth. However, over the last 150 years, the burning of fossil fuels has added more carbon dioxide to the atmosphere than can be removed by plants in photosynthesis. The concentration of carbon dioxide in the atmosphere has increased by about 25 percent in the last 100 years.

Carbon dioxide is called a greenhouse gas because it contributes to **global warming**. Global warming is the gradual increase in Earth's average temperature. The increasing levels of carbon dioxide in the atmosphere reflect heat coming from Earth's surface and direct it back toward the planet. This trapped heat results in global warming. Global warming may change global weather patterns and cause rising sea levels as polar ice caps melt.

Most scientists agree that global warming is caused by greenhouse gases such as carbon dioxide. They have recommended that steps be taken so that carbon dioxide does not continue to accumulate in the atmosphere. Such steps include the use of alternative energy sources to reduce the burning of fossil fuels, which is a major energy source.

Some scientists think we need more information before taking any action. They point to other factors that must be taken into account such as ocean temperatures and wind patterns that can affect Earth's temperature. However, all scientists do agree on one point—ecosystems are complex systems where living things interact in many different ways with their environment.

UNIT 6

Review

Darken the circle by the best answer.

1. Which category consists of only one species?

   (A) ecosystem

   (B) community

   (C) population

   (D) biome

2. A biome

   (A) is found in only one geographic area.

   (B) has distinct boundaries.

   (C) is characterized by the plants that grow there.

   (D) contains many more animal species than plant species.

3. Autotrophs are essential components of an ecosystem because they

   (A) represent the primary consumers.

   (B) break down organic matter so that it can be recycled.

   (C) form the top of most food chains.

   (D) are the primary producers.

4. In a food chain,

   (A) the number of organisms increases at each higher level.

   (B) each level contains only about 10 percent of the energy present in the previous level.

   (C) only the heterotrophs are included.

   (D) consumers serve as the base.

5. A food web differs from a food chain in that a food web

   (A) illustrates how one organism can depend on several sources of food for energy.

   (B) represents an energy flow that increases at each higher level.

   (C) does not show the feeding relationships among the organisms.

   (D) includes only the herbivores and carnivores.

6. Which process in the carbon cycle decreases the amount of carbon dioxide in the atmosphere?

   (A) decomposition

   (B) respiration

   (C) combustion

   (D) photosynthesis

7. Explain why food chains rarely consist of more than a few types of organisms.

   _____

   _____

   _____

8. Explain two ways that the burning of vegetation, such as trees, affects carbon dioxide levels in the atmosphere.

   _____

   _____

   _____

UNIT 6

Biomes

The table below lists the characteristics of the seven major biomes. Use the information in this table to answer the questions that follow.

Biome	Average yearly temperature range	Average yearly precipitation	Soil	Vegetation
Tundra	−26°C to 12°C	< 25 cm	moist, thin topsoil over permafrost; nutrient-poor; slightly acidic	mosses, lichens, dwarf woody plants
Taiga	−10°C to 14°C	35–75 cm	low in nutrients; highly acidic	needle-leafed evergreen trees
Temperate deciduous forest	6°C to 28°C	75–125 cm	moist; moderate nutrient levels	broad-leafed trees and shrubs
Temperate grassland	0°C to 25°C	25–75 cm	deep layer of topsoil; very rich in nutrients	dense, tall grasses in moist areas; short clumped grasses in drier areas
Desert	7°C to 38°C	< 25 cm	dry, often sandy; nutrient-poor	succulent plants and scattered grasses
Savanna	16°C to 34°C	75–150 cm	dry, thin topsoil; porous, low in nutrients	tall grasses, scattered trees
Tropical rain forest	20°C to 34°C	200–400 cm	moist; thin topsoil; low in nutrients	broad-leafed evergreen trees and shrubs

1. Which three biomes get the warmest?

_____

2. Which two biomes are the driest?

_____

3. Which biome has the least fluctuation in average yearly temperature?

_____

Biomes (cont'd.)

4. Which biome has the greatest fluctuation in average yearly temperature?

_____

5. What do a tundra and a tropical rain forest have in common?

_____

6. What do a tundra and a desert have in common?

_____

7. In which biomes does the average yearly temperature range not drop below freezing?

_____

8. Compared to a taiga, which biome receives about twice the amount of yearly precipitation?

_____

9. Explain why the grasses grow dense and tall in a temperate grassland.

_____

_____

_____

10. What do a temperate deciduous forest and a tropical rain forest have in common so that broad-leafed trees grow in both biomes?

_____

_____

_____

UNIT 6

A Food Chain

Examine the following food chain. Each arrow points to the organism that consumes the other organism. For example, cod eat krill. Use the information contained in the food chain illustration to answer the questions that follow.

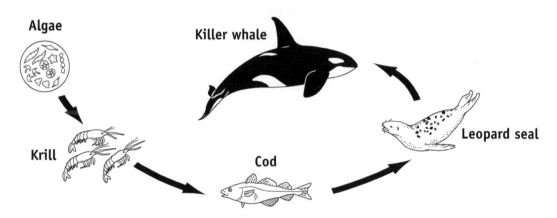

1. How many links make up this food chain? _____

2. Which organisms are the producers? _____

3. Which organism would be present in the smallest number? _____

4. Identify the herbivore(s) in this food chain. _____

5. Identify the carnivore(s) in this food chain. _____

6. Does this food chain contain any omnivores? Explain your answer.

_____

7. Predict what would happen to the krill population if the number of cod were significantly decreased because of fishing. Explain your answer.

_____

8. Would the decrease in the cod population affect the algae populations? Why or why not?

_____

9. Explain how a decrease in the cod population would affect higher levels in this food chain.

_____

UNIT 6

A Food Web

Examine the following diagram of a food web to answer the questions that follow.

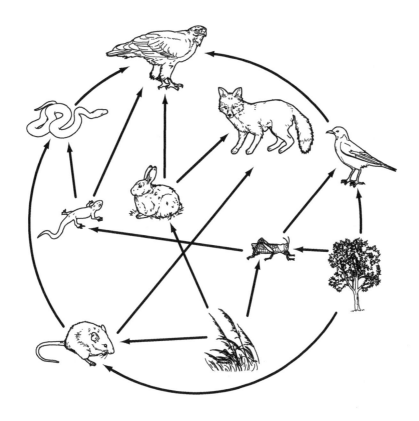

1. Identify one food chain that is part of this food web.

_____

2. Identify the producers.

_____

3. Identify the herbivores.

_____

4. Which organisms are found at the top level in this food web?

_____

UNIT 6

A Food Web (cont'd.)

5. What role does the bird play?

_____

_____

_____

6. Suppose the rabbit population was removed from this food web. Explain how this would affect the remaining organisms.

_____

_____

_____

_____

_____

7. Assume that the snake population suddenly starts to increase. What might have happened in this food web to cause such a change?

_____

_____

_____

_____

_____

UNIT 6

The Nitrogen Cycle

Use the following diagram of the nitrogen cycle to complete the passage below.

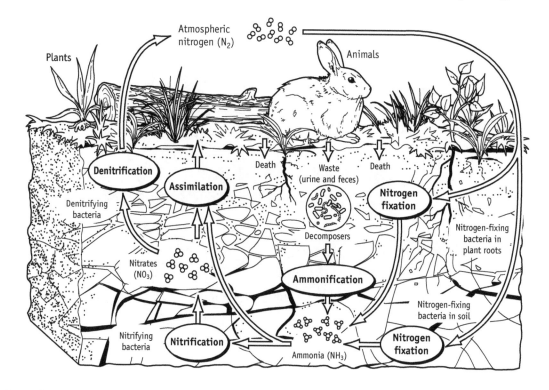

Nitrogen is cycled through an ecosystem by both plants and (1) _____. Decomposers

break down dead organisms and their waste products to release (2) _____ in a

process called (3) _____. Organisms called nitrifying bacteria convert this

(4) _____ into (5) _____ in a process called

(6) _____. These (7) _____ can then be used by plants

to make amino acids. The process of converting nitrogen in the atmosphere to ammonia is called

(8) _____. This process is carried out by bacteria that live in

(9) _____ and in (10) _____. Plants can absorb both

(11) _____ and (12) _____ from the soil, but animals

cannot. Animals obtain (13) _____ by eating plants and other organisms and then

digesting the proteins they contain.

UNIT 6

The Carbon Cycle

Use the following diagram of the carbon cycle to answer the questions that follow.

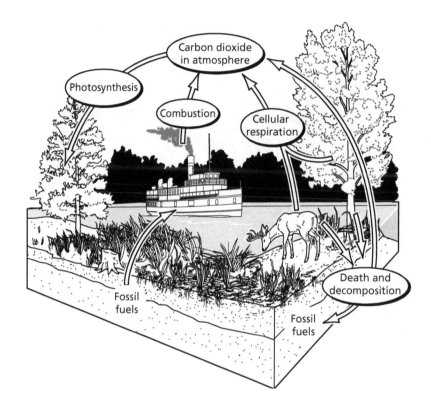

1. Identify the three processes that release carbon dioxide into the atmosphere.

_____

2. Identify the process that removes carbon dioxide from the atmosphere.

_____

3. Identify the process that has recently disrupted the balance that once existed in the carbon cycle.

_____

4. Explain how the cutting down of trees affects the carbon dioxide cycle.

_____

5. What do plants do with the carbon dioxide they remove from the atmosphere?

_____

UNIT 6

Global Warming

The following graph shows the changes in carbon dioxide concentration in the atmosphere for a twenty-year period, from 1974 to 1994. Use the information shown on this graph to answer the questions that follow.

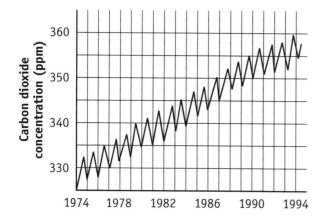

1. What general conclusion can you make from this graph?

_____

_____

_____

_____

2. The carbon dioxide concentrations fluctuate each year. They tend to drop each spring and summer. Explain why this happens.

_____

_____

_____

_____

3. In contrast, the carbon dioxide concentration tends to rise each fall. Explain why this happens.

_____

_____

_____

_____

4. Based on the graph, draw another graph to predict how Earth's average temperature changed over this twenty-year period.

Some organisms can only be seen with a microscope. These living things are called **microorganisms**. Microorganisms include bacteria, protozoa, algae, and slime molds. Although many of these organisms are very small, they are quite numerous and can be found everywhere on Earth. Bacteria live in sewage and at the bottom of swamps where there is no oxygen. One type of protozoan can thrive in human red blood cells where it can cause malaria, a deadly disease if not treated. This protozoan has caused more human deaths than any other organism in history. Algae come in various colors including green, red, brown, and gold. Slime molds have some characteristics like those found in mushrooms.

Key Terms

microorganism—a living thing that can be seen only with a microscope

retrovirus—a virus that contains reverse transcriptase that catalyzes the synthesis of DNA from RNA

lytic cycle—the reproductive cycle of a virus that destroys the host cell

lysogenic cycle—the integration and replication of viral nucleic acid along with the host cell's DNA

cilia—short, hairlike projections that function in locomotion

Viruses

At one time, viruses were also considered microorganisms. However, scientists discovered that viruses are quite different from living things. Today, viruses are considered to be nonliving particles. However, viruses can affect the functioning of cells that make up an organism. Viruses can even bring about the death of an organism.

The nature of viruses was not established until 1935. At that time, a scientist named Wendell Stanley obtained evidence that viruses might be chemicals rather than tiny cells. The following table compares a virus to a cell.

Characteristics of life	Virus	Cell
Growth	no	yes
Homeostasis	no	yes
Metabolism	no	yes
Mutation	yes	yes
Nucleic Acid	DNA or RNA	DNA
Reproduction	only within host cell	independently by cell division
Structure	nucleic acid core, protein covering, and, in some cases, an envelope	cytoplasm, cell membrane, cytoskeleton, and, in the eukaryotic cell, organelles

Notice that a virus consists of a protein coat that surrounds a nucleic acid core. The nucleic acid can be either DNA or RNA. Some RNA viruses are called **retroviruses** because they contain an enzyme that uses RNA to synthesize DNA. This is the reverse of the transcription process. As a result, this enzyme is called reverse transcriptase. The virus that causes AIDS is an example of a retrovirus.

One reason viruses are not considered living things is that they cannot reproduce by themselves. A virus can reproduce only by infecting a living cell. A virus attaches itself to the host cell. It then injects its nucleic acid into the host cell. The nucleic acid takes control of the cell and directs the synthesis of new viruses. These viruses eventually break open the cell, which disintegrates. The viruses can then infect other cells. This is known as the **lytic cycle**.

Some viruses can infect a host cell without destroying it. This is known as the **lysogenic cycle**. The nucleic acid that the virus injects becomes part of the cell's DNA. The viral DNA is replicated whenever the cell's DNA replicates. The viral DNA can remain part of the cell's DNA for days, months, or even years. Radiation or certain chemicals can cause the virus to leave the lysogenic cycle and enter the lytic cycle. This happens with the AIDS virus.

Bacteria

Bacteria are microscopic prokaryotes. They are classified into two separate kingdoms—Archaebacteria and Eubacteria. Archaebacteria are more ancient than the eubacteria. Archaebacteria include bacteria that convert hydrogen and carbon dioxide into methane gas. These bacteria live at the bottom of swamps and in the intestinal tracts of some animals, including cows and humans. Other archaebacteria live in environments with very high salt concentrations, such as the Great Salt Lake in Utah. Still other archaebacteria live in extremely acidic environments where temperatures exceed the boiling point of water. Such bacteria have been found on the ocean floor near volcanic vents miles below the surface.

Most bacteria are eubacteria. Most eubacteria have one of three basic shapes: (1) bacillus or rod-shaped; (2) coccus or sphere-shaped; and (3) spirillum or spiral-shaped. Rather than grouping eubacteria according to their shape, a more common method is to use a technique called the Gram stain. Some bacteria retain the Gram stain and appear purple under a microscope. These are called Gram-positive bacteria. Other bacteria do not retain the stain and appear pink under a microscope. These are called Gram-negative bacteria. This difference between bacteria is useful because Gram-positive bacteria react differently to antibiotics than Gram-negative bacteria. For example, penicillin is effective against Gram-positive bacteria, whereas streptomycin is effective against Gram-negative bacteria. This difference is critical in choosing the correct antibiotic to treat an illness.

All bacteria have a simple structure. They are composed of a cell wall, a cell membrane, and cytoplasm. The cell membrane is the only organelle

photosynthesis. However, algae do not have true roots, stems, or leaves and reproduce differently than plants. As a result, algae were reclassified and placed in the kingdom Protista. One of the best known algae is *Euglena*. This organism displays both animal-like and plant-like qualities. Euglena is animal-like because it does not have a cell wall. It is plant-like because it carries out photosynthesis.

Slime molds are an unusual group of organisms. They spend part of their life moving about searching for food. They also spend part of their life buried in the soil or attached to rotting logs or decaying leaves. Like all protists, slime molds are eukaryotes.

bacteria have. The cytoplasm contains a chromosome and ribosomes. Bacteria may be heterotrophic or autotrophic. Some autotrophic bacteria use sunlight as an energy source, just as green plants do. Interestingly, many bacteria cannot survive in the presence of oxygen. An example is the bacterium that causes tetanus. This is why a wound or cut is often treated with hydrogen peroxide. An enzyme in the blood breaks down the hydrogen peroxide to produce oxygen. The site of the wound then becomes saturated with oxygen, killing the bacteria that might otherwise cause tetanus.

Protists

A diverse collection of organisms make up the kingdom Protista. These organisms include protozoa, algae, and slime molds. Collectively, these organisms are called protists.

One of the best known and most thoroughly studied protozoa is *Paramecium*. This organism thrives in ponds and streams. Paramecia move with the help of short, hairlike projections called **cilia**. These cilia are arranged in rows across the cell membrane. They beat in synchronized strokes to propel the paramecia through the water. Paramecia are heterotrophs feeding upon decaying organic matter.

In contrast to protozoa, algae are autotrophs. Unlike protozoa, some algae can get quite large, reaching hundreds of feet in length. At one time, algae were classified in the same kingdom as plants because both types of organisms carry out

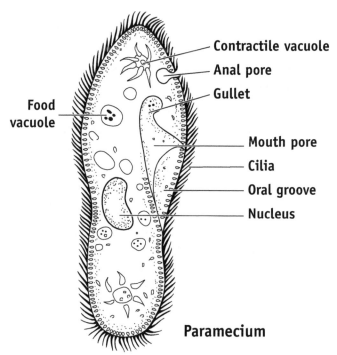

Food vacuole
Contractile vacuole
Anal pore
Gullet
Mouth pore
Cilia
Oral groove
Nucleus

Paramecium

UNIT 7

Review

Darken the circle by the best answer.

1. Viruses are not considered living things because they
   - Ⓐ do not contain genetic information.
   - Ⓑ contain proteins and nucleic acids but not carbohydrates.
   - Ⓒ cannot reproduce by themselves.
   - Ⓓ exhibit homeostasis.

2. During the lysogenic cycle, a virus
   - Ⓐ produces new viruses.
   - Ⓑ injects its DNA that then becomes part of the host cell's DNA.
   - Ⓒ destroys the host cell.
   - Ⓓ remains outside the host cell.

3. All bacteria
   - Ⓐ have a spiral shape.
   - Ⓑ require oxygen to survive.
   - Ⓒ are heterotrophic.
   - Ⓓ are prokaryotes.

4. Which is an organelle that is found in bacteria?
   - Ⓐ cell wall
   - Ⓑ cell membrane
   - Ⓒ nucleus
   - Ⓓ chromosome

5. Protozoa move through the water with the help of their
   - Ⓐ cilia.
   - Ⓑ chloroplasts.
   - Ⓒ cell wall.
   - Ⓓ contractile vacuole.

6. Unlike protozoa, algae
   - Ⓐ are heterotrophic.
   - Ⓑ are classified in the kingdom Plantae.
   - Ⓒ can be multicellular.
   - Ⓓ are not found as single-celled organisms.

7. What role do nucleic acids play in the grouping of viruses?

   _____

   _____

   _____

   _____

8. How do Gram-positive bacteria differ from Gram-negative bacteria?

   _____

   _____

   _____

   _____

   _____

   _____

UNIT 7

Viruses

The following illustrations show what happens after a virus attaches to a host cell and injects its nucleic acid. Use these illustrations to answer the questions that follow.

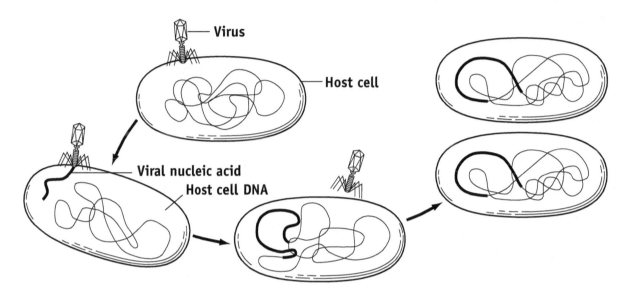

1. Do these illustrations represent the lytic cycle or the lysogenic cycle? Explain your answer.

_____

_____

2. What part of the virus remains outside the host cell?

_____

_____

3. Explain what happens to the viral nucleic acid when the host cell's DNA replicates.

_____

_____

The graph below shows how the number of viruses outside of a cell changes over time.

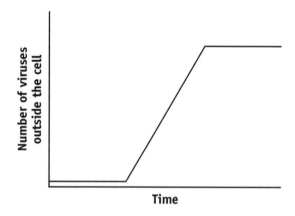

4. Describe what happened during the sharp rise in the graph.

_____

_____

Unit 7, Microorganisms
Biology, SV 0423-9

UNIT 7

Bacteria

Use the information contained in this passage to answer the questions below.

Bacteria and Disease

Various types of bacteria can cause disease. These organisms are known as pathogenic bacteria. Some pathogenic bacteria cause disease by producing poisons called toxins. These poisons cause fever, body aches, and weakness. An example of a bacterium that produces toxins is *Clostridium tetani*, which causes tetanus. Other pathogenic bacteria cause disease by damaging and destroying body tissues. The bacterium *Streptococcus pyrogenes* causes an upper respiratory infection known as strep throat. *Streptococcus* also secretes a digestive enzyme that allows other types of bacteria to spread to other tissues in the body.

The body has natural defenses to prevent bacterial infections. These defenses include the skin, which prevents bacteria from entering the body. If bacteria do invade the body, then other defenses are set in motion. The main internal defense consists of the immune system, which mounts an attack against the invading bacteria.

At times, the body's defenses are not sufficient to overcome pathogenic bacteria.

In such cases, an antibiotic may be required. Antibiotics are drugs that combat bacteria by interfering with their natural functions. For example, penicillin interferes with the formation of the cell wall. Streptomycin inhibits protein synthesis. Penicillin is known as a broad-spectrum antibiotic because it combats a variety of pathogenic bacteria.

In the past, antibiotics helped conquer bacterial diseases such as tuberculosis, syphilis, gonorrhea, and cholera. However, in recent years, bacteria have become increasingly resistant to antibiotics. Resistance to antibiotics develops when a few bacteria survive being exposed to the drug. These resistant bacteria have genes that make them immune to the drug. These bacteria survive and pass on their resistant genes to their offspring. Over time, the proportion of resistant bacteria increases. As a result, the antibiotic is no longer as effective. New drugs, and new strategies, will be needed to combat these resistant bacteria.

1. What are two ways in which bacteria cause disease? _____

_____

2. What would a narrow-spectrum antibiotic be? _____

_____

3. Why should a person be sure to follow a doctor's order to take all the antibiotic prescribed even though the person starts to feel better? _____

_____

UNIT 7

Protozoa

The following illustration shows a paramecium. Describe the function of each structure that is labeled.

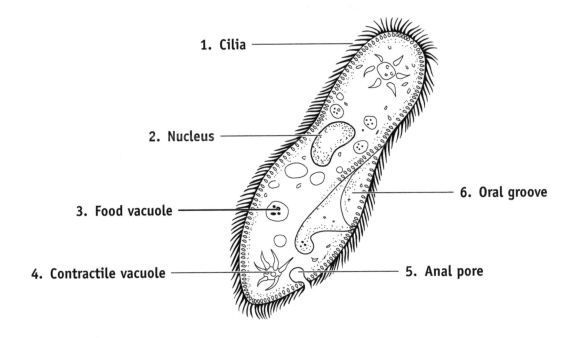

1. Cilia ————

2. Nucleus ————

6. Oral groove

3. Food vacuole ————

4. Contractile vacuole ————

5. Anal pore

1. cilia _____

2. nucleus _____

3. food vacuole _____

4. contractile vacuole _____

5. anal pore _____

6. oral groove _____

Unit 7, Microorganisms
Biology, SV 0423-9

UNIT 8

About 20 species of plants provide more than 90 percent of our food supply. Wheat is one of the world's most important food crops and is used to make breads, crackers, cereals, and pasta. Other food crops provide us with fruits, vegetables, nuts, oils, beverages, spices, sweeteners, herbs, flavorings, and snacks. An important group of plants includes root crops. The roots and underground stems of these plants provide us with potatoes, yams, sweet potatoes, radishes, beets, carrots, and turnips. Plants are also used as a source of medicines. Aspirin, the world's most widely used medicine, originally came from the bark of the white willow tree. Plants are also used to make clothing and the dyes to color them. Fossil fuels, such as coal, oil, and natural gas, come from plants that have been buried for millions of years. Plants have many other uses, including making

Key Terms

botany—the study of plants

vascular plant—a plant with vascular or conducting tissues, and true roots, stems, and leaves

nonvascular plant—a plant with neither vascular tissue nor true roots, stems, or leaves

seed—a plant embryo enclosed in a protective coat

cotyledon—a seed leaf in a plant embryo

adventitious root—an aboveground root that grows from a stem or leaf

xylem—the plant tissue that transports water and dissolved minerals upward

phloem—the plant tissue that transports organic compounds in both directions

palisade mesophyll—a layer of cells in a leaf directly beneath the surface

epidermis—a layer of cells that forms a protective covering on the outer surface

spongy mesophyll—a layer of loosely spaced cells in a leaf

stomata—tiny pores located on the underside of a leaf

guard cell—the cell that controls the opening and closing of stomata

pistil—the female reproductive structure in a flowering plant

ovary—the female structure that produces eggs

style—the structure that anchors the stigma to the ovary

stigma—the tip of the style where pollen grains are trapped

pollen grain—a male reproductive cell in plants

anther—the structure that produces cells that develop into pollen grains

filament—the structure that supports the anther

stamen—the male reproductive structure in a plant

sepal—the leaf-like parts on a flower

petal—the usually colorful leaf-like parts beneath the sepal

furniture, carpets, musical instruments, perfumes, soaps, and cosmetics. Plants also play a critical role in the water, carbon dioxide, and oxygen cycles.

Plant Classification

The study of plants is called **botany**. Scientists who study plants are called botanists. One area of interest to botanists is the classification of plants. All plants can be classified into two groups. One group includes the **vascular plants**. These plants have vascular or conducting tissues, and have true roots, stems, and leaves. The other group includes the **nonvascular plants**, which lack vascular tissue, true roots, stems, and leaves.

The nonvascular plants usually grow on land near streams and rivers. They are the most primitive types of plants. Because they lack vascular tissue, these plants are very small, growing no higher than 1–2 cm (less than 1 in.) in height. Common names of nonvascular plants are mosses and liverworts. Mosses are known as pioneer plants because they are often the first species to inhabit a barren area. They help to create a layer of soil, opening the area to other plants. Liverworts are unusual-looking plants that grow close to the ground.

The vascular plants can be subdivided into two groups. One group includes plants that do not produce **seeds**. The common names of these seedless, vascular plants are ferns, club mosses, and horsetails. Some of these plants have roots, while others have stems. These seedless, vascular plants dominated the Earth until about 200 million years ago. At that time, the second group of vascular plants evolved—those that produce seeds.

A seed is a plant embryo enclosed in a protective coat. Seeds provided plants with the opportunity to spread throughout terrestrial environments. If conditions are too hot or too cold or too dry or too wet, a seed will not start to grow or germinate. A seed will germinate only when conditions are just right. As a result, the chances of survival are much greater.

Plants that produce seeds can be further subdivided into two groups. One group, called

gymnosperms, bears their seeds in cones. The most familiar gymnosperms include pine, cedar, spruce, juniper, and fir trees. The tallest and most massive organisms on Earth are gymnosperms. These are the redwoods and giant sequoia trees.

The second group of seed plants includes plants called angiosperms. Although they evolved after gymnosperms, angiosperms quickly outnumbered them. One reason for their success was the ability of their seeds to produce mature plants, which in turn could produce new seeds, all in one growing season. In contrast, a gymnosperm may take ten or more years to reach maturity and produce seeds for a new generation.

Angiosperms can be subdivided into two groups— monocots and dicots. Monocots have only one **cotyledon**, which is a seed leaf in the plant embryo. Examples of monocots are lilies, orchids, bananas, corn, rice, onions, and wheat. Dicots have two cotyledons. Dicots include roses, maple trees, beans, and lettuce.

The classification of plants can be diagrammed as follows.

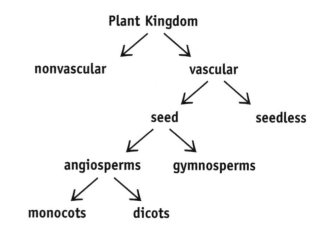

Plant Structures

Cells that work together to perform a specific function form a tissue. Tissues are organized into organs. Plants have three kinds of organs—roots, stems, and leaves. Roots, which normally grow underground, anchor the plant. Roots also serve two other functions. They absorb water and minerals. Roots also store carbohydrates and water. Familiar examples of plants with storage roots are carrots, turnips, and sweet potatoes.

The tips of roots grow downward through the soil. The tip is covered by a root cap which produces a slimy substance that allows the root to move through the soil more easily. Cells in the tip divide, elongate, and mature. Tiny root hairs cover the tip. These hairs increase the surface area of the root and therefore enable it to absorb more water and nutrients. Not all roots grow underground. Some roots grow from stems and leaves. These are called **adventitious roots**. For example, roots grow out from the stems of corn plants and help keep the plant upright.

The function of a stem is to support the leaves. Stems also transport water and materials between the roots and leaves. The transport of water and dissolved minerals occurs through a tissue called **xylem**. Transport through the xylem occurs from the roots to the stems and leaves. The transport of organic compounds, such as carbohydrates, occurs through a tissue called **phloem**. The transport through the phloem occurs in both directions depending on the plant's needs. If carbohydrates are needed in the leaves, then they will be transported up the stem through the phloem. If carbohydrates are to be stored in the roots, then they will be transported down the stem through the phloem.

Stems increase in thickness as additional bundles of xylem and phloem are added. The xylem that is added usually grows toward the inside of the stem. This added xylem is called wood. The phloem, which usually grows toward the outside of the stem, is part of the bark. The bark forms the protective coating of woody plants.

Leaves are the primary site of photosynthesis in most plants. The structure of leaf is adapted to its function. Examine the illustration of a cross section of a leaf below.

Most photosynthesis occurs in the mesophyll layer. Notice in the illustration that the mesophyll is organized into two layers. The **palisade mesophyll** is directly beneath the layer of cells that make up the **epidermis**. The epidermis is a protective layer of cells. Although the cells in the palisade layer are packed closely together, spaces between them allow the gases involved in photosynthesis to diffuse. The mesophyll cells are filled with chloroplasts, the site of photosynthesis. The lower layer, called the **spongy mesophyll**, allows gases to diffuse into and out of the leaf. Notice that vascular tissue, consisting of xylem and phloem, is also present.

The lower epidermis has tiny opening called **stomata**. Carbon dioxide, oxygen, and water pass through the stomata. If a plant is losing too much water, the stomata close. However, this closing shuts down photosynthesis because gases cannot diffuse into and out of the leaf. The opening and closing of the stomata is controlled by **guard cells**.

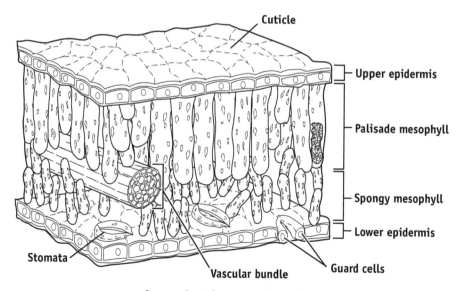

Cross Section of a Leaf

Another plant organ is found in angiosperms. This is the flower. A flower is the reproductive organ of a plant. Examine the following illustration of a flower.

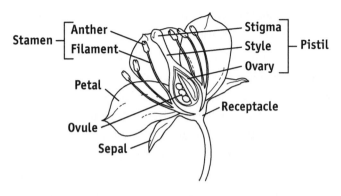

Flower

The female reproductive structures make up a **pistil.** The enlarged base is called the **ovary** where the eggs are formed. A **style** rises from the ovary. At the top of the style is the **stigma.** A stigma is sticky or has hairs to trap **pollen grains.** Pollen grains are the male reproductive cells of plants. Pollen is produced in the **anther.** The anther is attached to the plant by the **filament.** Together, the anther and filament make up the **stamen.** The pistil and stamen are protected by **sepals** and **petals.** The petals are the brightly colored parts of various land plants. The colorful petals help attract insects and birds that transport the pollen from one plant to another plant.

Fertilization in seed plants occurs when a pollen grain fertilizes an egg in the ovary. Actually, a double fertilization occurs in seed plants. As mentioned, one of these double fertilizations involves a pollen grain and an egg that unite and develop into a seed. The second fertilization occurs between another pollen grain and two egg cells. This second fertilization results in a tissue called the endosperm. The endosperm will provide nourishment for the seed as it germinates. This process of double fertilization is unique to angiosperms.

Many plants are easily grown from seeds. However, several conditions must be satisfied before a seed can start to grow or germinate.

First, there must be sufficient moisture. Water softens the seed coat and activates the enzymes inside the seed. These enzymes will break down the starches in the endosperm into simple sugars that the germinating seed will require for energy.

Second, the temperature must also be within a certain range. Some seeds will only germinate in mild weather. Other seeds, such as apple seeds, must be exposed to freezing temperatures for several weeks before they germinate.

Third, oxygen must be available so that the seed can carry out respiration. If seeds are buried too deeply in the ground, they may not be able to get enough oxygen. The seed may start to germinate, but it may stop growing when not enough oxygen is present so that respiration can occur.

Lastly, light may or may not be required for a seed to germinate. Some seeds can germinate quite well in the dark. However, many small seeds require light before they start to germinate. In such cases, the light can penetrate through the top layer of the soil to reach the seeds buried in the ground.

If satisfactory conditions are not met, then the seed will not germinate. Rather, the seed remains dormant. A seed can remain dormant for an extended period of time. Recently, a scientist was able to germinate seeds that had remained dormant for almost 1000 years.

UNIT 8

Review

Darken the circle by the best answer.

1. All vascular plants
   - (A) produce seeds.
   - (B) take several years to reach maturity.
   - (C) have seeds that contain two cotyledons.
   - (D) possess conducting tissue.

2. A rose is an example of a(n)
   - (A) nonvascular plant.
   - (B) gymnosperm.
   - (C) angiosperm.
   - (D) monocot.

3. Root hairs
   - (A) increase the surface area, allowing for more water absorption.
   - (B) store carbohydrates.
   - (C) are the sites where cells divide.
   - (D) grow only above ground.

4. In stems, xylem
   - (A) conducts carbohydrates in both directions.
   - (B) stores nutrients.
   - (C) is the site of photosynthesis.
   - (D) transports water and dissolved minerals upward to the leaves.

5. The mesophyll layer in a leaf
   - (A) is protected from the sun.
   - (B) is the site of photosynthesis.
   - (C) controls water loss from a leaf.
   - (D) controls the opening and closing of the stomata.

6. Which female structure in a flowering plant traps pollen grains?
   - (A) pistil
   - (B) stigma
   - (C) ovary
   - (D) anther

7. The colorful parts of flowering plants are the
   - (A) sepals.
   - (B) stamens.
   - (C) petals.
   - (D) filaments.

8. Explain why vascular plants are the most successful land plants.

   _____

   _____

9. Why is it an advantage for a leaf to have its stomata on the underside rather than on the surface?

   _____

   _____

UNIT 8

Plant Classification Puzzle

Unscramble each of the following sets of letters to form a word that deals with plant classification. Then use the circled letters to form the words for a plant.

1. desesesl   _ _ _ _ _ Ⓞ _ _

2. tanpl   _ _ Ⓞ _ _

3. yabnot   _ _ Ⓞ _ _ _

4. tocmoon   _ _ _ Ⓞ _ _ _

5. minkdog   Ⓞ _ _ _ _ _ _

6. tolocendy   _ _ _ _ Ⓞ _ _ Ⓞ

7. rampesgion   Ⓞ _ _ _ _ _ _ _ _ Ⓞ _

What a tiny seed may become

_ _ _   _ _ _   _ _ _ _ _

UNIT 8  Structure and Function of a Leaf

The following illustration shows a cross section of a leaf. Identify each numbered structure and describe its function.

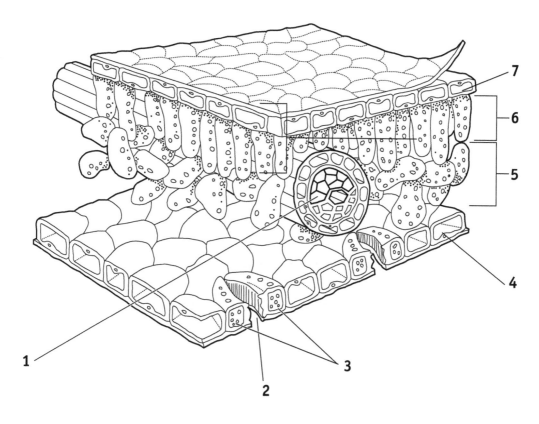

Structure	Function
1. _____	_____
_____	_____
2. _____	_____
_____	_____
3. _____	_____
_____	_____
4. _____	_____
_____	_____

Structure and Function of a Leaf (cont'd.)

5. _____   _____

   _____   _____

6. _____   _____

   _____   _____

7. _____   _____

   _____   _____

Answer the following question.

8. What adaptations does a leaf possess to carry out photosynthesis?

_____

_____

_____

_____

_____

_____

_____

_____

_____

_____

_____

_____

_____

_____

_____

_____

UNIT 8

Structure and Function of a Flower

The following illustration shows the parts of a flower. Identify each numbered structure and describe its function.

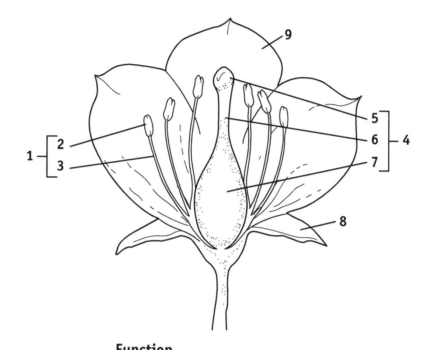

Structure	Function
1. _____	_____
2. _____	_____
3. _____	_____
4. _____	_____
5. _____	_____
6. _____	_____
7. _____	_____
8. _____	_____
9. _____	_____

UNIT 8

Plants vs. Humans

All living things must carry out certain functions and possess certain structures to survive, grow, and reproduce. The following chart illustrates how humans possess certain structures to carry out these critical functions. Fill in the plant structures that correspond to the human structures listed in the chart.

Function	Human Structure	Plant Structure
1. Gas exchange	lungs	_____
2. Circulation	blood vessels	_____
3. Water intake	mouth	_____
4. Energy intake	mouth	_____
5. Internal support	skeleton	_____
6. Energy storage	fat cells	_____
7. Energy conversion	mitochondria	_____

The kingdom Animalia includes two major groups of animals. One group consists of **vertebrates**, which are animals with a backbone. The other group consists of **invertebrates**, which are animals that do not have a backbone. Invertebrates account for more than 95 percent of all animal species alive today. Most of these invertebrates do not live on land, but rather in bodies of water such as the oceans, rivers, lakes, and streams.

All animals are heterotrophs composed of many cells that lack cell walls. Some animals contain a large number of cells. A human body, for example, consists of about 50 trillion cells. Groups of cells in most animals are specialized for a specific task. Some cells may be adapted for movement. Other cells may be specialized for reproduction, and so on. This specialization has enabled animals to evolve and adapt to many different environments.

Some animals reproduce asexually. **Asexual reproduction** is the production of offspring without the fusion of gametes or sex cells. However, most animals reproduce sexually. **Sexual reproduction** is the production of offspring through the fusion of gametes. Some animals carry out both types of reproduction. An example is an animal known as the hydra, an organism that has been extensively studied.

Key Terms

vertebrate—an animal with a backbone

invertebrate—an animal without a backbone

asexual reproduction—the production of offspring without the fusion of gametes

sexual reproduction—the production of offspring through the fusion of gametes

mutualism—a relationship where two organisms living together benefit

radial symmetry—a body structure where similar parts branch out in all directions from a central line

bilateral symmetry—a body structure which consists of two similar halves on either side of a central plane

setae—the bristle-like structures on an annelid's body

nephridia—the tubules through which an annelid eliminates wastes

exoskeleton—a rigid outer covering that protects the soft body parts

cuticle—a waxy layer that protects against dehydration

trachea—tiny air tubes in insects

metamorphosis—the stages of development through which an insect passes from fertilized egg to adult

Hydra

Hydras live in fresh water, such as ponds, streams, and lakes. They grow no more than 4 cm (1.6 in.) in length. Their slender bodies are usually white or brown. However, some hydras are green because of the algae that live inside their cells. The relationship between the hydra and the algae is an example of **mutualism**. This is a relationship where both animals benefit from living together. The algae are protected by living inside the hydra's cells. In turn, the hydras benefit from the organic compounds produced by the photosynthetic algae.

Hydras reproduce asexually during warm weather. Small buds develop on the outside of the hydra's body. The bud grows and eventually breaks off from the body. In cooler weather, hydras reproduce sexually. The cooler temperatures trigger the development of eggs and sperm. The same hydra may produce both types of gametes. When mature, the sperm are released into the water. They can fertilize eggs and develop into new hydras.

Hydras feed with the help of their tentacles. Cells on the tentacles are specialized for paralyzing and killing tiny organisms that swim or float by the hydra. When stimulated, these cells eject a long filament that usually has sharp tips and spines. These sharp objects may either pierce and poison the tiny organism or wrap around it. Nerve cells then coordinate the movement of the tentacles that push the tiny organism into the hydra's body cavity. A hydra's body displays **radial symmetry**. The term *symmetry* refers to a consistent overall pattern of body structure. In radial symmetry, similar parts branch out in all directions from a central line.

Earthworm

An invertebrate that displays a different type of symmetry is the earthworm. The earthworm displays **bilateral symmetry**. This type of symmetry consists of two similar halves on either side of a central plane. These two halves make up a right and left side.

Earthworms belong to a phylum called Annelida. The term *annelid* means "little rings." All the annelids in this phylum have a body consisting of many segments. An earthworm's body is made up of more than 100 segments. These segments make the animal look as if it were composed of a series of tiny rings.

Groups of segments are specialized for different functions. Segments near the front of an earthworm's body have a very simple brain and sense organs. A nerve cord extends from the brain and runs along the underside of the worm. This allows the brain to coordinate the body's activities. One such activity is movement. Each segment is covered with bristle-like structures called **setae**. An earthworm uses these setae to anchor its body in place. Muscles then contract to push the earthworm forward.

As it moves through the soil, an earthworm sucks soil into its mouth. The soil then passes through a tube that extends the length of the body, which also has the shape of a tube. For this reason, the body plan of an earthworm is referred to as a tube within a tube. As the soil passes through the inner tube, organic compounds are digested. Undigested materials pass out the anus at the end of the digestive tube. Wastes are also eliminated through tubules called **nephridia**. Each segment except the first three and the last one contains a pair of nephridia.

An earthworm produces both sperm and eggs. However, an earthworm's sperm cannot fertilize its own eggs. Two worms use their setae to keep their bodies in contact while they mate.

Grasshopper

About three-fourths of all animal species on Earth are insects. Insects have thrived for more than 300 million years. They owe their success to the many adaptations they possess to live in a wide variety of environments. Many of these adaptations can be seen in a grasshopper.

A major adaptation is the presence of an **exoskeleton**. An exoskeleton is a rigid outer covering that protects the soft body parts. However, an exoskeleton limits both the size and movement of an organism. The exoskeleton is covered by a waxy layer called a **cuticle**. The cuticle is also an adaptation to life on land because it protects the insect from dehydration.

Like that of most insects, the body of a grasshopper is divided into three parts: a head, thorax, and abdomen. The head contains the mouthparts and a pair of antennae. The thorax bears the three pairs of legs. The first two pairs are used for walking, while the third pair is used for jumping. The abdomen contains organs involved in digestion, excretion, and other functions.

Unlike earthworms, grasshoppers have a transport system known as an open circulatory system. In this system, blood is not always contained within a vessel, such as a vein or capillary. Instead, the blood percolates through open spaces in the animal's body.

Unlike most other animals, insects do not use their circulatory system to transport oxygen and carbon dioxide. To get oxygen and eliminate carbon dioxide, grasshoppers use a network of air tubes called **trachea**. The trachea open to the outside through tiny holes located on the sides of the thorax and abdomen.

Unlike hydras and earthworms, grasshoppers have separate sexes, as do all insects. Sperm are stored in a female's body until the eggs are released. The fertilized egg is then deposited in the soil. The young insect must pass through several stages of development before it reaches maturity. These stages of development are known as **metamorphosis**.

The hydra, earthworm, and grasshopper are classified as follows.

Hydra (*Chlorohydra viridissima*)
Kingdom: Animalia
Phylum: Cnidaria
Class: Hydrozoa
Genus: *Chlorohydra*
Species: *viridissima*
Other organisms that belong to the same phylum as hydra are jellyfish, corals, and sea anemones. The Portuguese man-of-war belongs to the same class as hydras.

Earthworm (*Lumbricus terrestris*)
Kingdom: Animalia
Phylum: Annelida
Class: Oligochaeta
Genus: *Lumbricus*
Species: *terrestris*
The phylum Annelida includes segmented worms that display bilateral symmetry. These worms include leeches.

Grasshopper (*Dissosteira carolina*)
Kingdom: Animalia
Phylum: Arthropoda
Class: Insecta
Genus: *Dissosteira*
Species: *carolina*
Cockroaches, praying mantises, and crickets are closely related to grasshoppers. They all belong to the same order known as orthoptera.

UNIT 9

Review

Darken the circle by the best answer.

1. Most animals are
   - Ⓐ heterotrophs.
   - Ⓑ vertebrates.
   - Ⓒ invertebrates.
   - Ⓓ organisms that live on land.

2. Hydras are animals that
   - Ⓐ display radial symmetry.
   - Ⓑ reproduce only sexually.
   - Ⓒ live in salt water.
   - Ⓓ have no specialized cells.

3. Earthworms are animals that
   - Ⓐ display radial symmetry.
   - Ⓑ are classified in the same phylum as hydra.
   - Ⓒ do not have specialized body parts.
   - Ⓓ use their muscles and setae to move through the soil.

4. Which applies to an earthworm but not to a hydra?
   - Ⓐ heterotroph
   - Ⓑ segmented
   - Ⓒ nerve cells
   - Ⓓ invertebrate

5. Grasshoppers are animals that have
   - Ⓐ both sexes in the same individual.
   - Ⓑ the same type of circulatory system as earthworms.
   - Ⓒ a skeleton on the outside of their body.
   - Ⓓ no structures specialized for movement.

6. Which applies to a grasshopper, but not to a hydra and an earthworm?
   - Ⓐ nerve cells
   - Ⓑ tentacles
   - Ⓒ setae
   - Ⓓ metamorphosis

7. Explain why most insects are small.

   _____

   _____

   _____

   _____

   _____

8. What is the difference between an open circulatory system and a closed circulatory system?

   _____

   _____

   _____

   _____

   _____

UNIT 9

Hydra

Use the following illustration of a hydra to answer the questions.

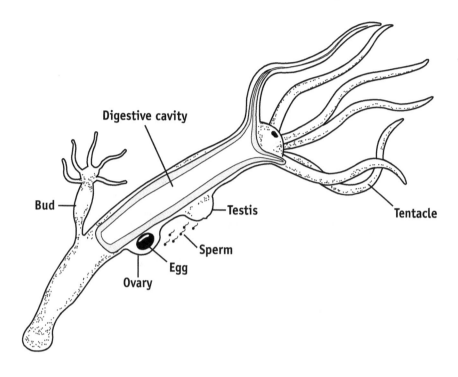

1. Describe how a hydra displays radial symmetry.

_____

_____

_____

2. How does the illustration above show that a hydra reproduces both asexually and sexually?

_____

_____

_____

3. What structures in the illustration above play a role in a hydra's feeding? Explain the role that these structures play.

_____

_____

_____

UNIT 9

Earthworm

Use the following illustration of an earthworm to answer the questions.

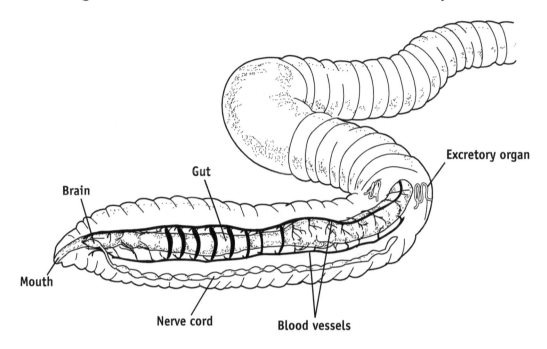

1. How does the illustration above show why an earthworm's body plan is referred to as a tube within a tube?

   _____

   _____

   _____

2. Where is an earthworm's brain located? Why is this location an advantage?

   _____

   _____

   _____

3. Notice that an earthworm has no specialized structures for respiration. Suggest how an earthworm takes in oxygen and eliminates carbon dioxide.

   _____

   _____

   _____

Unit 9

Grasshopper

Use the following illustration of a grasshopper to answer the questions.

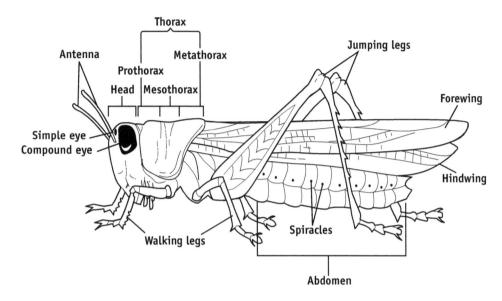

1. Which body part is divided into three smaller parts and what are their names?

_____

2. What three structures located on the head help the grasshopper sense its environment?

_____

3. Name the structures that help a grasshopper move.

_____

4. The spiracles are the tiny openings to the trachea. What function do the spiracles perform?

_____

5. What is the name of the structure that supports and protects the entire grasshopper's body?

_____

6. One set of wings is leathery, while the other set is much more delicate. Which set is leathery? Explain your answer.

_____

_____

UNIT 9

Classification II

Use the following chart to answer the questions. Each answer can be found in the letters A–E in the chart.

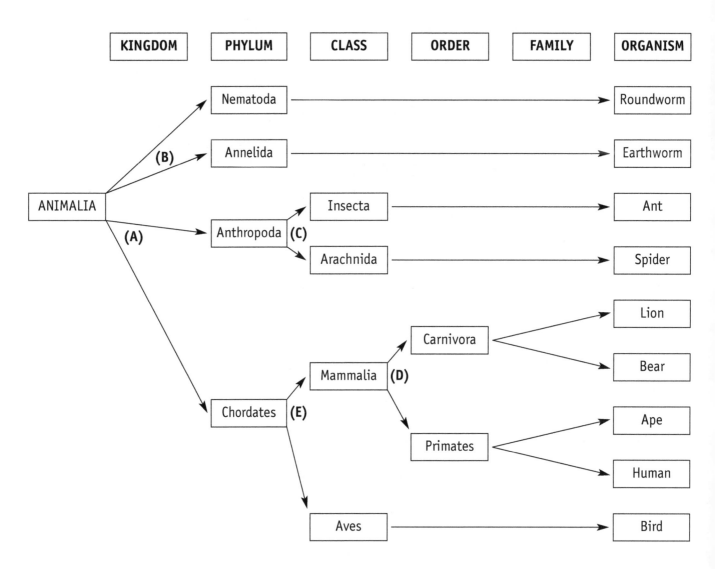

1. Separates animals with feathers from animals with hair _____

2. Separates animals with nails from animals with claws _____

3. Separates segmented worms from nonsegmented worms _____

4. Separates animals with exoskeletons from animals with endoskeletons, or internal skeletons _____

5. Separates the class to which grasshoppers belong _____

The Human Body

The human body has been called an incredible machine. An adult human body consists of about 50 trillion cells, which are organized into tissues. In turn, several tissues function together as an organ, such as the heart. Organs work together to form a system, such as the circulatory system. The functions of the different systems must be coordinated so that the human body works in an efficient manner. For an individual to survive and remain healthy, the organ systems must work together. This is no simple task when considering how many cells, tissues, organs, and systems are involved.

Key Terms

septum—the wall that divides the heart into right and left sides

atrium—an upper chamber of the heart

ventricle—a lower chamber of the heart

vein—a vessel that returns blood from all parts of the body to the heart

artery—a vessel that transports blood from the heart to all parts of the body

capillary—a vessel through which gases, nutrients, and wastes diffuse between the blood and cells

plasma—the liquid portion of the blood

hemoglobin—a protein in red blood cells that transports oxygen

platelet—a blood solid that is essential to blood clot formation

pharynx—a passageway for both air and food

epiglottis—a tiny flap that covers the trachea

trachea—a tube that connects the pharynx to the lungs

larynx—the voice box

bronchus—one of the two branches of the trachea that leads to the lungs

alveolus—one of the tiny air sacs in the lung

diaphragm—the muscle that controls the movement of the chest during breathing

endoskeleton—a skeleton that is located within the body

joint—the place where two bones meet

ligament—the tissue that connects two bones at a joint

cartilage—a tissue that protects bones against damage

skeletal muscle—a voluntary muscle that moves bones

tendon—the tissue that connects a skeletal muscle to a bone

smooth muscle—an involuntary muscle that is found in internal organs

cardiac muscle—the type of muscle that makes up the walls of the heart

esophagus—a tube that connects the mouth to the stomach

peristalsis—the muscular contractions that move food through the digestive system

bile—a substance produced by the liver that aids in lipid digestion

colon—the large intestine

urea—the nitrogenous waste product secreted by the kidney

Circulatory System

The heart is the main organ of the circulatory system. The heart's only function is to pump blood throughout the body. The illustration on the right shows the structure of the human heart.

A **septum** divides the heart into right and left sides. Each side is further divided into an upper chamber, called an **atrium**, and a lower chamber, called a **ventricle.** The right side pumps blood to the lungs. The left side pumps blood to the other parts of the body. Valves keep blood flowing in only one direction.

Blood returns from parts of the body other than the lungs and enters the right atrium. Blood returns to the heart through vessels called **veins.** Blood flowing through veins contains a high concentration

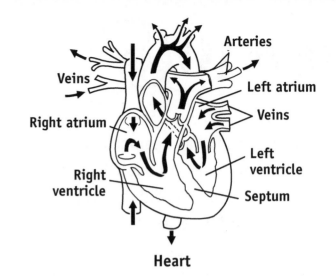

Heart

of carbon dioxide and a low concentration of oxygen. From the right atrium, blood passes to the right ventricle. The blood is then pumped out the

Key Terms cont'd.

ureter—the tube that connects the kidney with the urinary bladder

urethra—the tube that leads from the urinary bladder to the outside of the body

nephron—the functional unit of a kidney

glomerulus—the capillary network associated with a nephron

testis—the male reproductive structure where sperm are produced

vas deferens—the duct through which sperm pass out the testis

vagina—the female reproductive structure where sperm are deposited

uterus—the female reproductive structure where a fertilized egg develops

fallopian tube—the female reproductive structure where fertilization occurs

menstrual cycle—the 28-day cycle that involves changes in the female reproductive system

hormone—a chemical messenger secreted by an endocrine gland

neuron—a cell that transmits nerve signals

cerebrum—the portion of the brain that processes information and directs the appropriate responses

cerebellum—the portion of the brain involved in muscle coordination

medulla oblongata—the portion of the brain that controls certain involuntary actions

central nervous system—the brain and spinal cord

peripheral nervous system—the parts of the nervous system other than the brain and spinal cord

cell body—the part of the neuron that contains the nucleus

dendrite—an extension of a neuron that transmits a signal toward the cell body

axon—an extension of a neuron that transmits a signal away from the cell body

synapse—the tiny gap between two neurons

neurotransmitter—a chemical messenger that crosses a synapse

sensory receptor—a neuron specialized to detect a stimulus

reflex—an involuntary response to a stimulus

pulmonary artery to the lungs. **Arteries** are vessels that carry blood away from the heart.

In the lungs, carbon dioxide diffuses out of the blood and oxygen diffuses into the blood. This oxygen-rich blood returns to the heart through pulmonary veins. These veins enter the left atrium. The blood next enters the left ventricle. From here, the blood is pumped out a large artery called the aorta to all parts of the body except the lungs.

The walls of arteries are thick and muscular. This helps to keep the blood flowing in one direction. An artery branches to form smaller and smaller arteries. These vessels continue to branch to form tiny vessels called **capillaries**. The wall of a capillary is only one cell thick. As a result, gases and nutrients can easily diffuse across the wall of a capillary. Capillaries merge to form larger vessels. These vessels continue to merge to form a vein. In contrast to an artery, the wall of a vein is thin and less muscular. Veins have valves to keep the blood flowing back to the heart.

Blood consists of solids suspended in a liquid. The liquid is called **plasma**. The solids include red blood cells, which contain **hemoglobin**. Hemoglobin is a protein that transports oxygen in the blood. Blood solids also include white blood cells. While there is only one type of red blood cell, there are several types of white blood cells. These different types of white blood cells play a major role in fighting diseases and infections. Platelets are another blood solid. **Platelets** are essential to the formation of a blood clot.

Respiratory System

The function of the respiratory system is to get oxygen to the cells and remove the carbon dioxide they produce. The following illustration shows the structures that make up the respiratory system.

Air enters the body through the nasal passages where it is filtered and moistened. The air then passes to the **pharynx**, which is a passageway for both air and food. When food is swallowed, a tiny flap called the **epiglottis** presses down and shuts the opening to the air passage. When air is taken in, the epiglottis is in the upright position and allows air to pass into a tube called the **trachea**. The upper end of the trachea contains the **larynx**, or voice box.

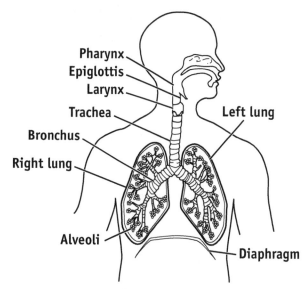

Respiratory System

The trachea branches into two **bronchi**. Each bronchus leads to a lung. The bronchi branch into smaller and smaller tubes. Eventually, the air reaches an **alveolus**, or tiny sac. Each lung contains nearly 300 million alveoli. Each alveolus is surrounded by a network of capillaries. Oxygen diffuses from the alveolus into the blood in the capillary. The oxygen is transported to the heart and then to other parts of the body for use in cellular respiration. Carbon dioxide diffuses from the blood in the capillary into the alveolus. The carbon dioxide then travels up the air passages and out the nasal passages.

The **diaphragm** is a muscle that controls the movement of the chest during breathing. The diaphragm contracts and moves downward to increase the volume of the chest cavity. This decreases the pressure inside the chest cavity. As a result, air from the atmosphere moves into the lungs. The diaphragm then relaxes and moves upward, forcing air out of the lungs.

Skeletal and Muscular Systems

The adult human body contains slightly more than 200 bones. These bones form the skeleton. Because this skeleton is located within the body, it is known as an **endoskeleton**. This endoskeleton serves several functions: (1) supports the body, (2) protects internal organs, (3) stores minerals such as calcium, and (4) works with muscles so that the body can move.

In addition, some bones produce both red blood cells and certain types of white blood cells.

The place where two bones meet is known as a **joint**. There are three types of joints in the human body—fixed, semimovable, and movable. A fixed joint prevents any movement of the two bones. Fixed joints are found in the skull. A semimovable joint permits only limited movement. For example, the semimovable joints hold the bones of the vertebral column or backbone in place. These joints allow the backbone to bend and twist. Movable joints allow a wide range of movements. An example is found in the shoulder joint which allows the bone in the upper arm to move up, down, forward, backward, as well as rotate in a complete circle.

The two bones of a joint are held in place by a **ligament**. The parts of the bones that come in contact with each other at a joint are covered with a softer tissue called **cartilage**. This cartilage prevents any wearing away of bones caused by rubbing against each other. Joints can become painful and swollen. One condition that causes this is arthritis. One type of arthritis develops when the cartilage at a joint becomes thinner. As a result, the bones rub against each other, causing pain.

Muscles make up the bulk of the body and account for about one-third its weight. Muscles are used for movement. This movement can be obvious, such as a person walking. However, the movement caused by muscles may not be obvious. Examples include heart muscles that contract to pump blood and muscles in the digestive tract that keep food moving.

The human body has three main types of muscles: skeletal, smooth, and cardiac. **Skeletal muscles** are responsible for moving parts of the body such as the arms, legs, and head. Because their contractions can be consciously controlled, skeletal muscles are known as voluntary muscles. Skeletal muscles are connected to a bone by a **tendon**.

Smooth muscles are found in the walls of the stomach, intestines, blood vessels, and other internal organs. Because most of their movements cannot be consciously controlled, smooth muscles are known as involuntary muscles.

Cardiac muscle makes up the walls of the heart. Cardiac muscle is unique in that it can beat in a rhythmic pattern.

Digestive System

The digestive system breaks down organic compounds into nutrients that cells can use. The digestive system begins in the mouth and winds its way through the body to the anus. This system consists of a tube that is divided into several organs. These organs include the esophagus, stomach, and intestines. Other organs secrete digestive enzymes that enter the digestive tract through ducts. These organs include the liver and pancreas. The following illustration shows the organs that are involved in digestion.

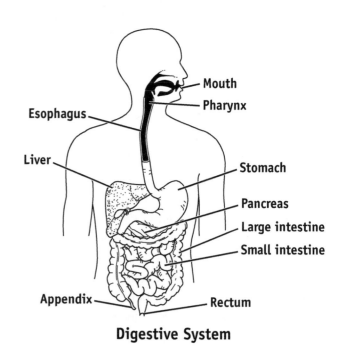

Digestive System

Digestion begins in the mouth. Chewing physically breaks down food into smaller pieces. Salivary glands secrete enzymes that enter the mouth to begin chemical digestion. These enzymes digest starches into disaccharides.

Food is then swallowed. The epiglottis prevents the food from entering the trachea. Instead, the food passes into the **esophagus** where it is moved along by muscular contractions and relaxations called **peristalsis**. No digestion occurs in the esophagus.

Digestion continues in the stomach. Muscles in the stomach walls churn and break the food into even smaller pieces. The stomach also releases enzymes that begin protein digestion.

The partially digested food passes next into the small intestine. The small intestine secretes enzymes that complete the digestion of carbohydrates and proteins and begin the digestion of lipids. Digestive enzymes also enter the small intestine through a duct from the pancreas. The liver secretes **bile** which also enters the small intestine through a duct. Bile is not an enzyme. However, bile does help in breaking down fats into smaller droplets, making it easier to digest them. The end products of digestion include amino acids, monosaccharides, fatty acids, and glycerol. These products are absorbed by the small intestine. The large intestine, or **colon**, absorbs a small amount of water from the undigested materials. The solid remnants are eliminated through the anus.

Excretory System

The main organ of the excretory system is the kidney. The kidneys eliminate nitrogenous wastes that are the byproducts of protein digestion. Water must also be eliminated to dissolve these wastes. The kidneys regulate the amount of water that is eliminated by the body. The nitrogenous wastes are eliminated as **urea**. Urea is made in the liver and then transported to the kidneys for elimination. The urea and water combine to form urine. The urine passes from each of two kidneys through a tube called the **ureter**. The ureters empty into the urinary bladder, which stores the urine until it is eliminated through the **urethra**.

Urine is made in structures called **nephrons**. Each kidney contains more than one million nephrons. If the nephrons from both kidneys were stretched out, they would extend for 80 km (50 mi). The artery to the kidney eventually branches into a capillary network called a **glomerulus**. Fluids from the blood pass into Bowman's capsule of the nephron. These fluids contain wastes, salts, nutrients, and water. The fluids pass from Bowman's capsule through the other parts of a nephron: the proximal convoluted tubule, the loop of Henle, and finally the distal convoluted tubule. Along the way, the nutrients are removed and returned to the bloodstream. Water and salts are also returned to the bloodstream should the body need them. If not, they too pass out of the body in the urine.

Reproductive System

Sperm are matured in the **testes**. They pass through a duct called the **vas deferens** and exit the body through the urethra in the penis. For fertilization to occur, sperm must be deposited in the **vagina** of the female reproductive system. The sperm must then travel up through the **uterus** and enter one of two **fallopian tubes**. A mature egg is released by an ovary and enters the fallopian tube where fertilization occurs.

The maturation of an egg is a complex process that spans about 28 days. This period of time is called a **menstrual cycle**. Several hormones are involved in the menstrual cycle. These hormones complete the maturation of an egg, cause the mature egg to be released from the ovary, and prepare the uterus should fertilization occur. The uterus is the site where the fertilized egg implants itself and undergoes development for about nine months. If fertilization does not occur, the thickened lining of the uterus is shed during a stage called menstruation, which lasts for about five days. The menstrual cycle then starts again.

Endocrine System

The endocrine system consists of glands that transmit chemical messages throughout the body. These chemical messages are called **hormones**. Hormones control the functioning of most organs in the body. Hormones are secreted by the glands into the blood stream. Each hormone has a specific target. For example, the pituitary gland secretes a hormone called follicle-stimulating hormone. This hormone targets the ovary to stimulate the maturation of an egg.

One gland of the endocrine system is sometimes referred to as the "master gland." This is the pituitary gland. This term is applied to the pituitary gland because it secretes nine major hormones that regulate the functioning of other endocrine glands. For example, the pituitary secretes a hormone that stimulates the thyroid gland to produce a hormone that affects growth and development.

The illustration on page 98 shows where the glands of the endocrine system are located throughout the body. Notice that some organs of the endocrine system are also part of other systems. For example, the stomach, which is part of the digestive system, also secretes hormones that are involved in digestion.

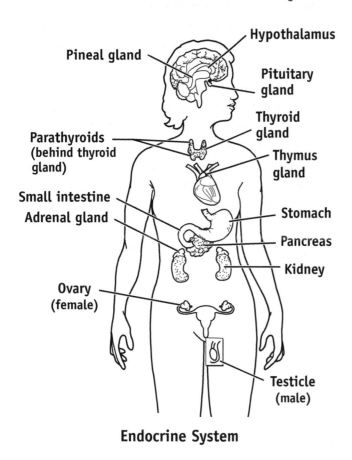

Endocrine System

Nervous System

The main organ of the nervous system is the brain. The brain actually has a relatively small mass compared to other body organs. An adult brain weighs about 1.5 kg, which is only 2 percent of total body weight. However, the brain does contain about 100 billion nerve cells, which are called **neurons**. The brain is responsible for overseeing the daily operations of the human body and for interpreting a vast amount of information it constantly receives.

The largest portion of the human brain is the **cerebrum**, which plays a major role in processing information and coordinating responses. Just below the cerebrum at the back of the skull is the **cerebellum**. This portion of the brain plays a vital role in coordinating muscle action. At the base of the brain is the **medulla oblongata.** This portion of the

brain coordinates involuntary actions, such as heart and respiratory rates. The medulla connects to the spinal cord. Together, the brain and spinal cord make up the **central nervous system.**

Neurons that extend out from the brain and spinal cord make up the **peripheral nervous system.** These neurons transmit signals both toward and away from the brain and spinal cord. For example, neurons from the senses, such as the eyes and ears, conduct signals they receive to the brain. Neurons in the brain interpret these signals and then send out the appropriate responses. For example, the ears may pick up the sounds of a barking dog, causing the brain to send signals to the muscles to start running.

All neurons have the same basic parts. A neuron consists of a **cell body** which contains the nucleus. Extending from the cell body are extensions called **dendrites**. A dendrite receives a signal from another neuron. Extending from the cell body in the opposite direction are extensions called **axons**. An axon transmits a signal away from the cell body and in the direction of another neuron, muscle, or gland. Neurons do not touch one another but are separated by a narrow gap called a **synapse**. Nerve signals are transmitted across a synapse with the help of chemical messengers called **neurotransmitters**.

Neurons that are specialized to detect a stimulus are known as **sensory receptors**. These neurons are found in high concentrations in the sense organs, which include the eyes, ears, nose, mouth, and skin. Each sense organ is highly specialized to carry out its job. For example, the tongue contains sensory receptors called taste buds. Nearly 10,000 taste buds are located on the tongue. Information they detect is sent to the brain where it is interpreted.

The nervous system sometimes carries out its job without involving the brain. Such actions are called **reflexes.** For example, someone stepping on a sharp object will automatically pull away his or her foot. In this case, the nerve signal travels from the foot to the spinal cord and directly back to the foot. Another example of a reflex response can be seen when the region below the knee is tapped sharply.

UNIT 10

Review

Darken the circle by the best answer.

1. Blood returning from the lungs enters the
   - Ⓐ left atrium.
   - Ⓑ left ventricle.
   - Ⓒ right atrium.
   - Ⓓ right ventricle.

2. Which structure contains blood with a high carbon dioxide content?
   - Ⓐ aorta
   - Ⓑ left atrium
   - Ⓒ pulmonary vein
   - Ⓓ pulmonary artery

3. A muscle is connected to a bone by a(n)
   - Ⓐ tendon.
   - Ⓑ ligament.
   - Ⓒ joint.
   - Ⓓ endoskeleton.

4. Identify the organ where protein digestion begins.
   - Ⓐ mouth
   - Ⓑ esophagus
   - Ⓒ stomach
   - Ⓓ liver

5. The functional unit of a kidney is known as a
   - Ⓐ glomerulus.
   - Ⓑ loop of Henle.
   - Ⓒ convoluted tubule.
   - Ⓓ nephron.

6. Fertilization occurs in the
   - Ⓐ vas deferens.
   - Ⓑ fallopian tube.
   - Ⓒ uterus.
   - Ⓓ vagina.

7. The chemical messengers of the endocrine systems are
   - Ⓐ nerve impulses.
   - Ⓑ hormones.
   - Ⓒ digestive enzymes.
   - Ⓓ red blood cells.

8. Which is *not* a part of a neuron?
   - Ⓐ cell body
   - Ⓑ axon
   - Ⓒ synapse
   - Ⓓ dendrite

9. What two systems regulate the activities of all the systems that make up the human body?

   _____

10. Select any two systems and show how they are interrelated.

   _____

   _____

   _____

   _____

UNIT 10

The Circulatory System

The following illustration shows blood flow through the human body. Identify each of the numbered structures.

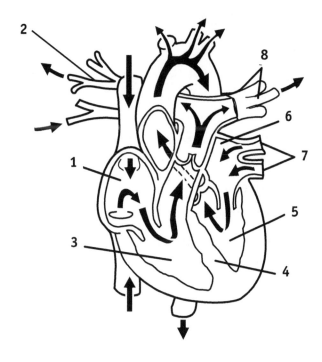

1. _____

2. _____

3. _____

4. _____

5. _____

6. _____

7. _____

8. _____

9. Which structure prevents blood from mixing between the two sides of the heart?

_____

10. How are the pulmonary veins different from all other veins in the body?

_____

_____

11. Explain why the walls of the lower chambers of the heart are thicker and more muscular than the walls of the upper chambers.

_____

_____

12. Explain why an artery cannot be defined as a blood vessel that transports oxygenated blood.

_____

UNIT 10

The Respiratory System Word Search

Use the information and descriptions below to find the words in the following puzzle.

1. the tiny air sac in the lung (8 letters)

2. the gas the respiratory system gets rid of (13 letters)

3. the voice box (6 letters)

4. the gas the respiratory system takes in (6 letters)

5. there are two, with one going to each lung (8 letters)

6. the muscle that controls breathing (9 letters)

7. the main organ of the respiratory system (4 letters)

8. the common passage for food and air (7 letters)

9. the type of blood vessel where gases are exchanged in the lungs (9 letters)

10. the structure that prevents choking (10 letters)

11. commonly known as the windpipe (7 letters)

12. the common term for what we breathe in (3 letters)

13. the process of moving air into and out of the lungs (9 letters)

14. the process by which gases are exchanged in the lungs (9 letters)

15. the first place air enters the body (4 letters)

```
E K I F E Q E S R A H N T M N P H G E R
Q G T R E W F L E E T T S X V M N S X D
F U Q L E R Q P H B L R R A B I U V M M
T S O A P O T Y S O L T S P H A L W E D
H C N R I D S M A O E S B T N H O H E L
N E C Y G F Y N G S T R A C H E A N X A
E E E N L A E N I A E E D P T Z D P N H
E D I X O I D N O B R A C F N E G Y X O
W I G Z T T P S E B S H R E P O O S I S
H F E J T E S H D E N E P U I R U S L H
Z F B M I E Y R A L L I P A C G Y F D V
O U L R S B T E Q R E S I A I W A Q H O
L S U L O E V L A A Y L S H R D I E E M
E I N M M N N P Z T P N J S M F U M E A
R O G E D H C I L X E F X O P F J C L B
E N R R I R T H H D E G S R A B D R C L
L T M R I E R E U D E R E E A J U O U L
U A E A H I X G E S O N S N E R H I S P
S D S O G B I M E T N S S M L O D F O H
T Q P D S E I A S G R T N R I E T N K G
```

UNIT 10  Skeletal and Muscular Systems

Match the description in column I with the structure in column II. A description in column I may match more than one item listed in column II. Also, an item in column II can be used more than once.

Column I

1. connects bone to bone _____

2. place where two bones meet _____

3. bone rubbing against bone _____

4. under voluntary control _____

5. connects bone to muscle _____

6. allows for body movements _____

7. prevents movement _____

8. protects internal organs _____

9. found in the walls of the heart _____

10. under involuntary control _____

11. protects bones _____

12. found in the skull _____

Column II

A. fixed joint

B. cardiac muscle

C. skeletal muscle

D. tendon

E. cartilage

F. muscular system

G. smooth muscle

H. joint

I. arthritis

J. ligament

K. skeletal system

Select the term that does not belong with the others and explain your choice.

13. tendon, fixed joint, skeletal muscle, arm bone _____

_____

14. provides support, produces red blood cells, stores minerals, contracts and relaxes

_____

_____

UNIT 10

The Digestive System

The following illustration shows the organs of the digestive system. Identify each of the numbered structures and describe its function(s).

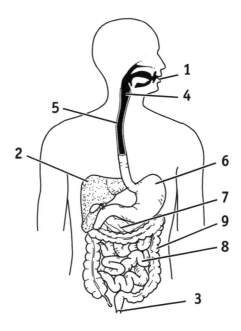

Structure   **Function**

1. _____   _____

2. _____   _____

3. _____   _____

4. _____   _____

5. _____   _____

6. _____   _____

7. _____   _____

8. _____   _____

9. _____   _____

Unit 10, The Human Body
Biology, SV 0423-9

UNIT 10

The Excretory System

Label each structure in the following illustration of the excretory system.

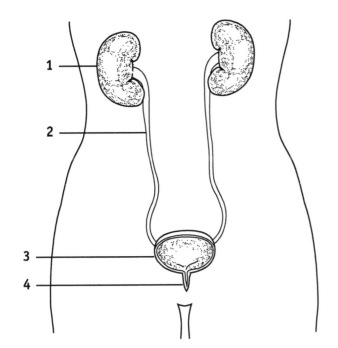

1. _____

2. _____

3. _____

4. _____

Label each structure in the following illustration of a nephron.

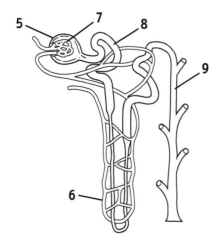

5. _____

6. _____

7. _____

8. _____

9. _____

UNIT 10    The Reproductive System

The following illustration shows the changes that occur during the menstrual cycle. Answer the questions below by referring to this illustration.

1. At what point during the cycle is the egg released from the ovary?

   _____

2. Which hormone shows the greatest increase just prior to this point?

   _____

3. Which hormone is present at the highest level toward the end of the cycle?

   _____

4. Changes in the uterus are illustrated at the bottom of the graph. How do high levels of estrogen and progesterone during the luteal phase affect the uterus?

   _____

   _____

   _____

   _____

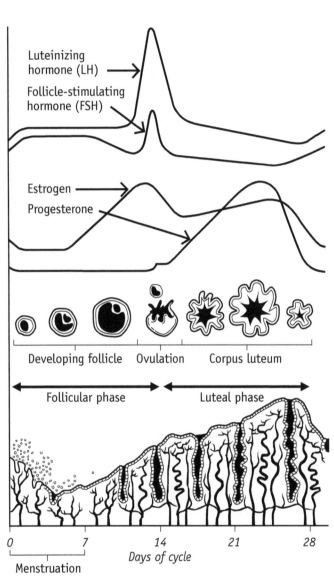

5. Describe what is happening to the uterus after day 28 of the cycle.

   _____

   _____

6. What must occur for the changes after day 28 not to happen to the uterus?

   _____

UNIT 10

The Endocrine System

The following table lists most of the endocrine glands, the hormones they produce, and their functions. Answer the questions below based on the information in this table.

Glands	Hormone	Function
Adrenal glands Cortex	aldosterone cortisol	maintains salt-and-water balance regulates carbohydrate and protein metabolism
Medulla	epinephrine, norepinephrine	initiate body's response to stress and the "fight-or flight" response to danger
Ovaries	estrogen progesterone	regulates female secondary sex characteristics maintains growth of uterine lining
Pancreas (islets of Langerhans)	glucagon insulin	stimulates release of glucose stimulates absorption of glucose
Parathyroid glands	parathyroid hormone	increases blood calcium concentration
Pineal gland	melatonin	regulates sleep patterns
Testes	androgens (testosterone)	regulates male secondary sex characteristics
Thymus gland	thymosin	stimulates a type of white cell formation
Thyroid gland	thyroxine	increases cellular metabolic rates

1. Which hormones are involved in controlling blood sugar?

_____

2. Which endocrine gland is activated if you are suddenly startled and become frightened?

_____

3. Can a person who is having trouble sleeping have a hormonal problem? Explain your answer.

_____

4. Which endocrine gland listed in the table above is also part of the digestive system?

_____

The Endocrine System (cont'd.)

5. How might a malfunctioning thymus gland affect a person's health?

_____

6. How do the parathyroid glands affect the calcium level in the bones?

_____

7. What hormones begin to be secreted at puberty?

_____

Answer the questions.

8. Describe how the endocrine system and the nervous system are similar.

_____

_____

_____

_____

9. Why might damage to the pituitary gland be considered more serious than damage to the other endocrine glands?

_____

_____

_____

_____

UNIT 10  The Nervous System Crossword

ACROSS

3. Part of the central nervous system

7. Transmits signal away from the cell body

8. Organelle located in the cell body

9. Nerve cell

11. Coordinates muscle activity

14. Something you do without thinking about it

DOWN

1. Largest portion of the human brain

2. Sense organ with taste

3. Where two neurons meet

4. Type of response controlled by the medulla

5. Transmits signal toward the cell body

6. What a nerve may stimulate in time of danger

10. What a neurotransmitter is

12. Amazingly small for such an important job

13. Site where you can see many sensory receptors

GLOSSARY

adaptation—a trait or behavior that increases an organism's chances of survival (p. 48)

adventitious root—an aboveground root that grows from a stem or leaf (p. 77)

aerobic respiration—respiration with oxygen (p. 16)

allele—an alternative form of a gene (p. 27)

alveolus—one of the tiny air sacs in the lung (p. 95)

amino acid—a molecule that is the building block of a protein (p. 15)

anaerobic respiration—respiration without oxygen (p. 16)

anther—the structure that produces cells that develop into pollen grains (p. 78)

anticodon—a sequence of three nitrogen-containing bases in tRNA that pairs with the three-base codon in mRNA (p. 40)

artery—a vessel that transports blood from the heart to all parts of the body (p. 95)

asexual reproduction—the production of offspring without the fusion of gametes (p. 85)

ATP—adenosine triphosphate; the main compound that cells use for energy (p. 16)

atrium—an upper chamber of the heart (p. 94)

autotroph—an organism that converts light energy into chemical energy (p. 17)

axon—an extension of a neuron that transmits a signal away from the cell body (p. 98)

bilateral symmetry—a body structure which consists of two similar halves on either side of a central plane (p. 86)

bile—a substance produced by the liver that aids in lipid digestion (p. 97)

binary fission—the process where a prokaryotic cell splits to form two cells (p. 5)

biome—a geographic land area characterized by particular types of animals and plants (p. 57)

biosphere—the area on and around Earth where life exists (p. 56)

botany—the study of plants (p. 76)

bronchus—one of the two branches of the trachea that leads to the lungs (p. 95)

Calvin cycle—the pathway in photosynthesis where carbon dioxide is changed into an organic compound (p. 17)

capillary—a vessel through which gases, nutrients, and wastes diffuse between the blood and cells (p. 95)

carbohydrate—a compound that is composed of carbon, hydrogen, and oxygen in the proportion of 1:2:1 (p. 14)

cardiac muscle—the type of muscle that makes up the walls of the heart (p. 96)

carnivore—a consumer that eats other consumers (p. 57)

cartilage—a tissue that protects bones against damage (p. 96)

cell—the smallest unit of a living thing that can carry on all the processes of life (p. 3)

cell body—the part of the neuron that contains the nucleus (p. 98)

central nervous system—the brain and spinal cord (p. 98)

cerebellum—the portion of the brain involved in muscle coordination (p. 98)

cerebrum—the portion of the brain that processes information and directs the appropriate responses (p. 98)

cilia—short, hairlike projections that function in locomotion (p. 70)

GLOSSARY

codominance—a situation where both alleles for a gene are expressed in a heterozygous individual (p. 28)

codon—a sequence of three nitrogen-containing bases in mRNA that specifies a particular amino acid (p. 40)

colon—the large intestine (p. 97)

community—all the living things in an ecosystem (p. 57)

consumer—a heterotroph that obtains energy by feeding upon other organisms or organic waste materials (p. 57)

cotyledon—a seed leaf in a plant embryo (p. 76)

crossing-over—the process in meiosis where chromosomes exchange genetic information (p. 6)

cuticle—a waxy layer that protects against dehydration (p. 87)

cytoplasm—the part of a cell between the nucleus and the cell membrane (p. 4)

decomposer—an organism that breaks down wastes and complex molecules in dead organisms into simpler molecules (p. 57)

dehydration synthesis—the process of joining smaller molecules to form a larger one accompanied by the loss of a water molecule (p. 15)

dendrite—an extension of a neuron that transmits a signal toward the cell body (p. 98)

deoxyribonucleic acid (DNA)—the nucleic acid that stores the genetic information as genes on a chromosome (p. 38)

diaphragm—the muscle that controls the movement of the chest during breathing (p. 95)

diffusion—the movement of substances from an area of high concentration to an area of lower concentration (p. 6)

dihybrid cross—a cross between individuals that involves two traits (p. 27)

diploid—the chromosome number in most cells of an organism (p. 6)

dominant—referring to a factor that masks another factor for the same trait (p. 27)

ecology—the study of the interactions between organisms and their environment, which includes both living and nonliving components (p. 56)

ecosystem—all the organisms and the nonliving environment found in a particular place (p. 56)

electron transport chain—the third and final pathway in respiration, taken only if oxygen is available (p. 16)

embryo—a fertilized egg cell that has started to divide and grow (p. 47)

endoskeleton—a skeleton that is located within the body (p. 95)

energy—the capacity for doing work (p. 13)

enzyme—a chemical substance that speeds up the rate of a chemical reaction (p. 16)

epidermis—a layer of cells that forms a protective covering on the outer surface (p. 77)

epiglottis—a tiny flap that covers the trachea (p. 95)

esophagus—a tube that connects the mouth to the stomach (p. 96)

eukaryote—a cell that contains a cell membrane, a nucleus, and other organelles (p. 4)

exoskeleton—a rigid outer covering that protects the soft body parts (p. 87)

fallopian tube—the female reproductive structure where fertilization occurs (p. 97)

fermentation—the pathway pyruvic acid follows in the absence of oxygen (p. 16)

GLOSSARY

filament—the structure that supports the anther (p. 78)

food chain—the pathway through which energy flows in an ecosystem (p. 57)

food web—the interconnected food chains in an ecosystem (p. 58)

fossil—a trace of a long-dead organism (p. 46)

genetics—the field of biology that focuses on how characteristics are transmitted from parents to offspring (p. 26)

genotype—the genetic makeup of an organism (p. 27)

global warming—the increase in Earth's average temperature caused by greenhouse gases (p. 58)

glomerulus—the capillary network associated with a nephron (p. 97)

glycolysis—the first pathway in respiration where glucose is changed into pyruvic acid (p. 16)

guard cell—the cell that controls the opening and closing of stomata (p. 77)

haploid—the chromosome number in a mature sex cell (p. 5)

hemoglobin—a protein in red blood cells that transports oxygen (p. 95)

herbivore—a consumer that eats a producer (p. 57)

heterotroph—an organism that obtains energy by eating other organisms (p. 17)

heterozygous—the condition where both alleles of a pair are different (p. 27)

homeostasis—the process where a cell or organism maintains a stable internal environment (p. 6)

homologous structure—a structure that has a different function in various organisms but shares a common ancestry (p. 47)

homozygous—the condition where both alleles of a pair are alike (p. 27)

hormone—a chemical messenger secreted by an endocrine gland (p. 97)

hypertonic—of two solutions, the solution with a higher solute concentration (p. 6)

hypotonic—of two solutions, the solution with a lower solute concentration (p. 6)

incomplete dominance—a situation where two or more alleles influence the phenotype, which is in between that of the parents (p. 28)

invertebrate—an animal without a backbone (p. 85)

isotonic—the condition in which the concentration of solutes outside a cell equals the concentration inside the cell (p. 6)

joint—the place where two bones meet (p. 96)

Krebs cycle—the second pathway in respiration, taken only if oxygen is available (p. 16)

larynx—the voice box (p. 95)

law of independent assortment—the independent segregation of the factors that control different traits (p. 27)

law of segregation—the segregation, or separation, of two factors for the same trait when a gamete forms (p. 27)

ligament—the tissue that connects two bones at a joint (p. 96)

lipid—a compound that is composed of a high proportion of carbon and hydrogen with a much smaller proportion of oxygen. Lipids include fats, oils, and waxes. (p. 15)

lysogenic cycle—the integration and replication of viral nucleic acid along with the host cell's DNA (p. 69)

GLOSSARY

lytic cycle—the reproductive cycle of a virus that destroys the host cell (p. 69)

macromolecule—a very large molecule, such as a protein or nucleic acid (p. 47)

medulla oblongata—the portion of the brain that controls certain involuntary actions (p. 98)

meiosis—the process of cell division which forms mature sex cells (p. 5)

menstrual cycle—the 28-day cycle that involves changes in the female reproductive system (p. 97)

messenger RNA—the nucleic acid that carries the genetic information from the DNA in the nucleus to the cytoplasm (p. 39)

metabolism—the sum of all life processes occurring within an organism (p. 13)

metamorphosis—the stages of development through which an insect passes from fertilized egg to adult (p. 87)

microorganism—a living thing that can be seen only with a microscope (p. 68)

mitosis—the process of cell division in eukaryotic cells (p. 5)

monohybrid cross—a cross between individuals that involves one trait (p. 27)

mutualism—a relationship where two organisms living together benefit (p. 86)

natural selection—the theory that organisms best suited to their environment reproduce more successfully than others (p. 48)

nephridia—the tubules through which an annelid eliminates wastes (p. 86)

nephron—the functional unit of a kidney (p. 97)

neuron—a cell that transmits nerve signals (p. 98)

neurotransmitter—a chemical messenger that crosses a synapse (p. 98)

nonvascular plant—a plant with neither vascular tissue nor true roots, stems, or leaves (p. 76)

nucleic acid—a large organic molecule that stores and carries genetic information in the cell (p. 38)

omnivore—a consumer that is both an herbivore and a carnivore (p. 57)

organelle—a cell component that performs a specific function (p. 4)

organic compound—a compound based on the element carbon (p. 13)

organism—a living thing (p. 3)

osmosis—the movement of water molecules across a membrane from an area of higher concentration to an area of lower concentration (p. 6)

ovary—the female structure that produces eggs (p. 78)

palisade mesophyll—a layer of cells in a leaf directly beneath the surface (p. 77)

pedigree—a family history that shows individuals who display a particular trait and those who do not display the trait (p. 29)

peripheral nervous system—the parts of the nervous system other than the brain and spinal cord (p. 98)

peristalsis—the muscular contractions that move food through the digestive system (p. 96)

petal—the usually colorful leaf-like parts beneath the sepal (p. 78)

pharynx—a passageway for both air and food (p. 95)

phenotype—the expression of the genotype of an organism (p. 27)

phloem—the plant tissue that transports organic compounds in both directions (p. 77)

photosynthesis—the process that converts light energy into chemical energy (p. 17)

GLOSSARY

pistil—the female reproductive structure in a flowering plant (p. 78)

plasma—the liquid portion of the blood (p. 95)

platelet—a blood solid that is essential to blood clot formation (p. 95)

pollen grain—a male reproductive cell in plants (p. 78)

polypeptide—a long chain of amino acids (p. 16)

polysaccharide—a large molecule made by linking many individual carbohydrates (p. 14)

population—all the members of a species that live in the same area (p. 57)

producer—an autotrophic organism that captures energy to make organic molecules (p. 57)

prokaryote—a single-celled organism with only one organelle, a cell membrane (p. 4)

protein—a large molecule made from amino acids (p. 15)

Punnett square—a way to show the possible outcomes of a genetic cross (p. 27)

pyruvic acid—a key intermediate in respiration (p. 16)

radial symmetry—a body structure where similar parts branch out in all directions from a central line (p. 86)

recessive—referring to a factor that is masked by another factor for the same trait (p. 27)

reflex—an involuntary response to a stimulus (p. 98)

replication—the process of copying DNA (p. 39)

respiration—a series of chemical reactions that break down organic compounds and transfer the energy they contain into a form that cells can use (p. 16)

retrovirus—a virus that contains reverse transcriptase that catalyzes the synthesis of DNA from RNA (p. 69)

ribonucleic acid—the molecule that is responsible for assembling proteins based on the genetic information contained in DNA (p. 39)

ribosomal RNA—the nucleic acid that combines with proteins to form the ribosomes (p. 39)

saturated fat—a lipid that contains only single bonds between its carbon atoms (p. 15)

seed—a plant embryo enclosed in a protective coat (p. 76)

sensory receptor—a neuron specialized to detect a stimulus (p. 98)

sepal—the leaf-like parts on a flower (p. 78)

septum—the wall that divides the heart into right and left sides (p. 94)

setae—the bristle-like structures on an annelid's body (p. 86)

sex chromosome—a chromosome that carries the genes that determine an individual's sex (p. 28)

sexual reproduction—the production of offspring through the fusion of gametes (p. 85)

skeletal muscle—a voluntary muscle that moves bones (p. 96)

smooth muscle—an involuntary muscle that is found in internal organs (p. 96)

solute—a substance that dissolves in a solution (p. 6)

species—a group of organisms that can mate with one another and produce fertile offspring (p. 48)

spongy mesophyll—a layer of loosely spaced cells in a leaf (p. 77)

stamen—the male reproductive structure in a plant (p. 78)

stigma—the tip of the style where pollen grains are trapped (p. 78)

GLOSSARY

stomata—tiny pores located on the underside of a leaf (p. 77)

style—the structure that anchors the stigma to the ovary (p. 78)

synapse—the tiny gap between two neurons (p. 98)

tendon—the tissue that connects a skeletal muscle to a bone (p. 96)

testis—the male reproductive structure where sperm are produced (p. 97)

trachea—tiny air tubes in insects (p. 87); a tube that connects the pharynx to the lungs in humans (p. 95)

transcription—the process by which genetic information is copied from DNA to RNA (p. 39)

transfer RNA—the nucleic acid that transports amino acids to the ribosomes where they will be assembled into a protein (p. 39)

translation—the process of assembling amino acids based on the information in mRNA (p. 40)

transpiration—the process by which plants release water into the atmosphere (p. 58)

unsaturated fat—a lipid that contains one or more double bonds between its carbon atoms (p. 15)

urea—the nitrogenous waste product secreted by the kidney (p. 97)

ureter—the tube that connects the kidney with the urinary bladder (p. 97)

urethra—the tube that leads from the urinary bladder to the outside of the body (p. 97)

uterus—the female reproductive structure where a fertilized egg develops (p. 97)

vagina—the female reproductive structure where sperm are deposited (p. 97)

vas deferens—the duct through which sperm pass out the testis (p. 97)

vascular plant—a plant with vascular or conducting tissues, and true roots, stems, and leaves (p. 76)

vein—a vessel that returns blood from all parts of the body to the heart (p. 94)

ventricle—a lower chamber of the heart (p. 94)

vertebrate—an animal with a backbone (p. 85)

vestigial structure—a structure present in an organism that has no function (p. 47)

X-linked trait—a trait whose alleles are located only on the X chromosome (p. 29)

xylem—the plant tissue that transports water and dissolved minerals upward (p. 77)

ANSWER KEY

Unit 1

Page 7
Review

1. C
2. B
3. A
4. C
5. B
6. B
7. D
8. Possible answers include ribosomes, rough endoplasmic reticulum, and Golgi apparatus.
9. Mitosis involves one division that produces two cells, each of which contains the same number and kinds of chromosomes as found in the original cell. In contrast, meiosis involves two divisions that produce four cells, each of which contains half the number of chromosomes as found in the original cell. In addition, the cells produced by meiosis contain new chromosome combinations.

Pages 8–9
Animal and Plant Cells

1. C and F
2. G
3. H
4. K
5. J
6. B
7. L
8. M
9. A
10. C
11. D
12. E
13. I
14. B
15. K
16. mitochondrion—A chloroplast, which is a plastid, contains a pigment.
17. cell wall—Both animals and plant cells contain ribosomes, a nucleus, and a cell membrane. However, only plant cells contain a cell wall.
18. chromosome—The Golgi apparatus, smooth endoplasmic reticulum, and lysosome are organelles found in the cytoplasm. A chromosome is not an organelle and is found in the nucleus.
19. Because of its high energy requirement, a muscle cell contains many mitochondria.
20. A plant cell is a eukaryotic cell because it contains a variety of organelles.

Page 10
Mitosis

1. anaphase; 3; each member of a chromosome pair moves toward opposite ends of the cell
2. prophase; 1; chromosomes shorten and become visible
3. metaphase; 2; chromosomes are aligned in the center of the cell
4. telophase; 4; chromosomes reach opposite ends of the cell as the cell membrane forms a furrow

Page 11
Mitosis and Meiosis

1. mitosis
2. meiosis
3. both
4. meiosis
5. mitosis
6. meiosis
7. mitosis
8. meiosis
9. meiosis
10. both
11. both
12. mitosis
13. both
14. meiosis
15. meiosis
16. both
17. mitosis
18. both

Page 12
Diffusion and Osmosis

1. Salt is in higher concentration on the left side of the membrane and therefore will diffuse to the right side.
2. Water is in higher concentration on the right side of the membrane and therefore will move by osmosis to the left side.

ANSWER KEY cont'd.

3. The figure must be redrawn to show equal numbers of water molecules and salt particles on each side.

4. A correct answer includes any drawing that shows more water molecules outside the cell and fewer salt particles inside the cell. The only structure that must be included is a cell membrane to show the boundary of an animal cell or a cell wall to show the boundary of a plant cell.

Unit 2

Page 18

Review

1. C
2. A
3. D
4. A
5. B
6. D
7. C

8. Both carbohydrates and lipids are organic compounds. However, carbohydrates contain C, H, and O in a nearly 1:2:1 proportion, while lipids contain a much higher proportion of C and H relative to O.

9. The equation has to be rewritten in reverse because the products of respiration are used as the reactants in photosynthesis.

Page 19

Organic Chemistry Word Search

1. amino acid
2. cholesterol
3. enzyme
4. protein
5. water
6. carbohydrate
7. dipeptide
8. lipid
9. saturated fat
10. cellulose
11. energy
12. metabolism

Page 20

Organic Chemistry

1.

CH_2OH

2.

$$H-\overset{|}{\underset{|}{C}}-O-\overset{O}{\overset{||}{C}}-C_{15}H_{31}$$

$$H-\overset{|}{\underset{|}{C}}-O-\overset{O}{\overset{||}{C}}-C_{15}H_{31}$$

$$H-\overset{|}{\underset{|}{C}}-O-\overset{O}{\overset{||}{C}}-C_{15}H_{31}$$

$$H$$

Answer Key
Biology, SV 0423-9

ANSWER KEY cont'd.

3.

Page 21

Proteins

serine — alanine — cysteine — glycine — phenylalanine

Page 22

Enzymes

1. 37°C
2. 98°C
3. Enzyme B because it functions best at 98°C, which is near the boiling point of water (100°C).
4. Increasing the temperature has a greater effect. For example, increasing the temperature from 40°C to 50°C causes enzyme A's activity to drop drastically while an increase of 10° does not have as great an effect.

Page 23

Respiration

1. $C_3H_6O_3$
2. C_2H_5OH
3. $C_6H_{12}O_6 + 6O_2 \longrightarrow 6CO_2 + 6H_2O + 38ATP$
4. efficiency of anaerobic respiration = 2 × 12 kilocalories/686 kilocalories × 100% = 3.5%
5. efficiency of aerobic respiration = 38 × 12 kilocalories/686 kilocalories x 100% = 66.5%

Page 24

Photosynthesis

1. autotrophs
2. energy
3. light
4. chemical
5. chloroplast
6. light
7./8. ATP; NADPH
9. light reactions
10./11. dark reactions; Calvin cycle
12. carbon dioxide
13. carbohydrates
14. oxygen
15. light
16./17. carbon dioxide; water
18./19. oxygen; carbohydrates
20. respiration
21. autotrophs
22./23. autotrophs/heterotrophs

ANSWER KEY cont'd.

Page 25

Respiration and Photosynthesis

1. photosynthesis
2. respiration
3. both
4. respiration
5. photosynthesis
6. respiration
7. photosynthesis
8. both
9. respiration
10. both
11. both
12. photosynthesis
13. photosynthesis
14. respiration
15. photosynthesis
16. photosynthesis
17. respiration
18. respiration
19. photosynthesis

Unit 3

Page 30

Review

1. D
2. B
3. A
4. C
5. D
6. B
7. A Punnett square shows all the possible outcomes and the probability of each outcome. It does not state that any one outcome is certain to occur.
8. In the case of an X-linked recessive trait, a male needs only one allele to show the condition whereas a female needs two recessive alleles.

Page 31

Review

1. gene
2. allele
3. pedigree
4. genetics
5. dominant
6. phenotype
7. chromosome
8. hemophilia
9. homozygous

Who started all this? Gregor Mendel

Page 32

Monohybrid Crosses

1.

	B	b
b	Bb	bb
b	Bb	bb

Bb = black
bb = brown

2.

Parental			F₁		
	P	P		P	p
p	Pp	Pp	P	PP	Pp
p	Pp	Pp	p	Pp	pp

PP and **Pp** = purple
pp = white

3.

Parental			F₁		
	B	B		B	b
b	Bb	Bb	b	Bb	bb
b	Bb	Bb	b	Bb	bb

A brown color in the F₁ can be obtained only if the black color guinea pig is heterozygous.

ANSWER KEY cont'd.

Page 33
Dihybrid Crosses

1. GGSS and ggss

2.

	GS	GS
gs	GgSs	GgSs
gs	GgSs	GgSs

100% green, short

All the offspring possess a dominant allele for both traits, therefore resulting in only one phenotype.

3. SSBB, SsBb, SSBb, and SsBB

4.

	SB	Sb	sB	sb
SB	SSBB	SSBb	SsBB	SsBb
Sb	SSBb	SSbb	SsBb	Ssbb
sB	SsBB	SsBb	ssBB	ssBb
sb	SsBb	Ssbb	ssBb	ssbb

5. $\frac{9}{16}$ = short, black hair

   $\frac{3}{16}$ = short, brown hair

   $\frac{3}{16}$ = long, black hair

   $\frac{1}{16}$ = long, brown hair

Page 34
Incomplete Dominance and Codominance

1. RR = red; WW = white; RW = pink

2.

	R	R
R	RR	RR
W	RW	RW

RR = red
RW = pink

3. His decision is incorrect because a cross between plants with pink flowers can produce plants with red flowers and plants with white flowers as shown by the following Punnett square.

	R	W
R	RR	RW
W	RW	WW

RR = red
RW = pink
WW = white

4. Yes, actually a horse with roan color can be produced from parents which both have roan coat color as shown by the Punnett cross in the following answer.

5.

	R	R′
R	RR	RR′
R′	RR′	R′R′

RR = red
RR′ = roan
R′R′ = white

Page 35
Blood Types

1. An individual cannot have an ABO blood type because an individual can possess only two alleles for this trait.

2.

	I^A	i
I^B	$I^A I^B$	$I^B i$
i	$I^A i$	ii

ii = Type O

3.

	I^A	I^B
i	$I^A i$	$I^B i$
i	$I^A i$	$I^B i$

no type $I^A I^B$

ANSWER KEY cont'd.

4.

	i	i
I^B	I^{B}i	I^{B}i
I^B	I^{B}i	I^{B}i

	i	i
I^B	I^{B}i	I^{B}i
i	ii	ii

5.

	I^A	I^B
I^A	I^{A}I^A	I^{A}I^B
I^B	I^{A}I^B	I^{B}I^B

25% probability of type A blood

Page 36
Sex-Linkage

1. A father passes his X chromosome on to his daughters. Therefore, any X-linked trait cannot be passed on to his sons.

2.

	X^H	Y
X^H	X^{H}X^H	X^{H}Y
X^h	X^{H}X^h	X^{h}Y

X^{H}X^H = normal female
X^{H}X^h = carrier
X^{H}Y = normal male
X^{h}Y = hemophiliac male

3.

	X^c	Y
X^c	X^{c}X^c	X^{c}Y
X^c	X^{c}X^c	X^{c}Y

X^{c}X^c = carrier
X^{c}Y = normal male

Page 37
Pedigrees

1. This genetic disorder is inherited as a recessive trait. If this disorder were caused by a dominant allele, then every individual with this condition would have a parent with this disorder.

2. This genetic disorder is not X-linked. If this disorder were X-linked, then the father would also have the condition because he passes on his X chromosome to all his daughters, and not just one daughter.

3.

D = normal
d = disorder

	d	d
D	Dd	Dd
D	Dd	Dd

100% normal; all carriers

Unit 4
Page 41
Review

1. C
2. C
3. B
4. A
5. C
6. D
7. A double helix refers to the structure of DNA, which consists of two strands wound around each other like a spiral staircase.
8. The ribosomes are the sites where mRNA attaches to direct protein synthesis in the cytoplasm.

Page 42
DNA and Replication

1. The structure of a DNA molecule is referred to as a double helix, which is similar in shape to a spiral staircase.
2. A — T and G — C
3. A copy must be made of each DNA molecule so that each cell produced by mitosis receives a complete set of genetic instructions.
4.

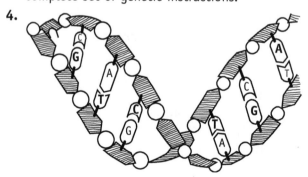

ANSWER KEY cont'd.

5.

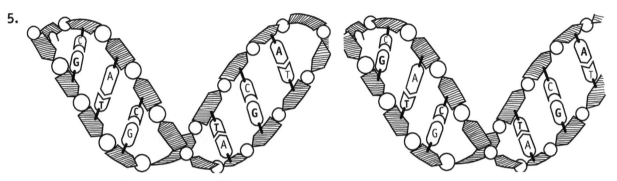

Two identical molecules of DNA are formed. Both molecules are identical to the original DNA.

Page 43
RNA and Transcription

1. deoxyribose
2. ribose
3. uracil
4. thymine
5. phosphate
6. messenger RNA
7. nucleus
8. cytoplasm
9. transfer RNA
10. ribosomes
11. ribosomal RNA
12. transcription
13. double helix
14. complementary
15. guanine
16. adenine
17. cytosine

Page 44
Protein Synthesis

1.

C—C—G—G—A—U—G—U—A—C—C—G—G—U—U—U—C—C—A—G—U—G—A—A—U—U—A—A—G

2. tyrosine—arginine—phenylalanine—proline—valine—aspargine

Page 45
Genetic Engineering

1. Genetic engineering has resulted in a DNA molecule that has been formed by recombining the DNAs from two different species.
2. The human growth hormone can be used to treat people who are abnormally short. Genetic engineering is an efficient way to produce large quantities of the hormone.
3. The gene for pest resistance can be isolated from the plant. Genetic engineering can then be used to insert the gene into the DNA of the other plant species.

ANSWER KEY cont'd.

Unit 5

Page 49
Review
1. D
2. B
3. A
4. C
5. C
6. D
7. Possible answers include the fossil record, homologous structures, vestigial structures, similarities in early embryonic development, and comparison of macromolecules.
8. According to the theory of natural selection, organisms that are better adapted to their environment have a better chance of survival and therefore of reproducing and having offspring.

Pages 50–51
Earth's History
1. 208 million years ago
2. about 141 million years (Dinosaurs first arose about 208 million years ago and became extinct some 67 million years ago.)
3. The Jurassic period was the time dinosaurs diversified and populated the Earth.
4. Tertiary period
5. about 163 million years (Seed plants arose 245 million years ago while land plants first appeared 408 million years ago.)
6. They both are times of mass extinctions.
7. Precambrian
8. Eocene
9. Devonian
10. Carboniferous

Page 52
Evolution: Facts and Theory
1. F; A vestigial organ serves no purpose.
2. T
3. F; Natural selection states that a portion of the organisms in a population have the adaptations to survive in their environment.
4. F; Organisms that are adapted to survive are more likely to interbreed and produce offspring.
5. F; Similarities between the early stages of embryo development of two different organisms are an indication that they share a common ancestor.
6. F; The term "survival of the fittest" is often associated with the theory of natural selection. The term "survival of the fittest" refers to the survival of the organisms that possess the adaptations needed to survive.
7. T
8. F; The scientific explanation as to how evolution occurs is a theory.
9. T

Page 53
Classification I
Answers will vary. Students should recognize that developing a classification system is not a simple task, even when only ten objects are involved. They can appreciate the task that Linnaeus faced when he classified thousands of organisms. You can ask students to repeat their effort, this time using more objects.

Page 54
Classification: Dichotomous Keys
a. English oak
b. shingle oak
c. Lombardy poplar
d. live oak
e. redbud
f. chestnut oak

ANSWER KEY cont'd.

Page 55
Biological Diversity Crossword

Across
3. vestigial
6. Animalia
8. order
9. evolution
11. genus
12. neck
14. class
15. adaptation
17. homologous
20. embryo
22. heterotroph
23. autotroph
24. Plantae

Down
1. fossil
2. family
4. dinosaurs
5. breed
7. natural selection
10. Linnaeus
13. kingdom
16. theory
18. ammonia
19. species
21. methane

Unit 6
Page 59
Review
1. C
2. C
3. D
4. B
5. A
6. D
7. A food chain is usually short because only about 10 percent of the energy is transferred from one level to the next higher one. After about three to four transfers, there is not enough energy to support another level.
8. Burning vegetation means less photosynthetic activity and more combustion. Both result in an increased level of carbon dioxide in the atmosphere.

Pages 60–61
Biomes
1. desert, savanna, and tropical rain forest
2. tundra and desert
3. tropical rain forest
4. tundra

5. Both a tundra and a tropical rain have moist, thin topsoils that are low in nutrients.
6. Both a tundra and a desert have an average yearly precipitation of less than 25 cm.
7. temperate deciduous forest, desert, savanna, and tropical rain forest
8. savanna
9. The temperature does not drop below freezing, there is adequate precipitation, and the soil is very rich in nutrients.
10. Both biomes are moist. As a result, the leaves can be broad and not narrow or needle-like to conserve water.

Page 62
A Food Chain
1. five
2. algae
3. killer whale
4. krill
5. cod, leopard seal, and killer whale
6. No, because none of the organisms are shown as being both an herbivore and a carnivore.
7. The krill population would increase as there would be fewer cod to feed on them.
8. Yes, the higher number of krill would result in a decrease in the algae populations.
9. With fewer cod, the leopard seal population would decline, followed by a decline in the killer whale population.

Pages 63–64
A Food Web
1. Several answers are possible including: grass → grasshopper → lizard → snake → hawk.
2. grass and trees
3. rabbits, grasshoppers, birds, and mice
4. hawks and foxes
5. The bird is an omnivore, serving as both an herbivore by eating seeds and a carnivore by eating grasshoppers.

ANSWER KEY cont'd.

6. If the rabbit population were removed, the grasses might increase, providing more food for the grasshoppers and mice. However, elimination of the rabbit population would mean less food for the foxes and hawks, which would then have to depend more on their other sources, such as mice and snakes.

7. A sudden increase in the snake population might be the result of an increase in their food supply (lizard and mice populations) and/or a decrease in their predators (hawk population).

Page 65
The Nitrogen Cycle
1. animals
2. ammonia
3. ammonification
4. ammonia
5. nitrates
6. nitrification
7. nitrates
8. nitrogen fixation
9./10. plant roots; soil
11./12. ammonia; nitrates
13. nitrogen

Page 66
The Carbon Cycle
1. cellular respiration, combustion, and decomposition
2. photosynthesis
3. combustion of fossil fuels
4. The loss of trees means that less carbon dioxide will be removed from the atmosphere for photosynthesis and less will be added as a result of cellular respiration.
5. Plants use carbon dioxide to produce carbohydrates in photosynthesis.

Page 67
Global Warming
1. Despite seasonal fluctuations, the carbon dioxide concentration in the atmosphere showed a steady increase from 1974 to 1994.
2. Leaves present on trees in spring and summer carry our photosynthesis, which reduces atmospheric carbon dioxide concentration.
3. As leaves drop in fall, photosynthetic activity declines, raising the carbon dioxide concentration. As the weather cools, more fossil fuels are used for heating.
4. The graph should show the same overall increase for temperature as this graph shows for carbon dioxide concentration.

Unit 7
Page 71
Review
1. C   2. B
3. D   4. B
5. A   6. C
7. Viruses can be grouped depending on whether they contain DNA or RNA.
8. Bacteria that retain the Gram stain are Gram-positive and appear purple under a microscope. Those bacteria that do not retain the Gram stain are Gram-negative and appear pink.

Page 72
Viruses
1. The illustrations show the lysogenic cycle because the viral DNA is integrated with the host cell DNA.
2. The protein coat or shell remains outside the host cell.
3. The viral DNA is replicated along with the host cell DNA.
4. The sharp rise on the graph corresponds to the stage in the lytic cycle when the viruses break open the host cell and emerge.

ANSWER KEY cont'd.

Page 73
Bacteria

1. Bacteria cause disease by producing toxins and by damaging and destroying body tissues.
2. A narrow-spectrum antibiotic would be one that is effective against only one or perhaps a few bacteria.
3. Failure to finish the antibiotic may allow resistant bacteria to survive. They will then reproduce and pass on their resistance to their offspring.

Page 74
Protozoa

1. cilia: used for locomotion
2. nucleus: contains the genetic information and directs the cell's activities
3. food vacuole: site where organic molecules are broken down
4. contractile vacuole: excretes excess water
5. anal pore: eliminates undigested materials
6. oral groove: site where food particles enter

Unit 8
Page 79
Review

1. D   2. C   3. A   4. D
5. B   6. B   7. C

8. Vascular plants have the most efficient system for gathering and transporting water, dissolved minerals, and organic compounds.
9. The stomata are not as easily clogged by dust or rain.

Page 80
Plant Classification Puzzle

1. seedless
2. plant
3. botany
4. monocot
5. kingdom
6. cotyledon
7. angiosperm

What a tiny seed may become: an oak tree

Pages 81–82
Structure and Function of a Leaf

1. vascular bundle (xylem and phloem); conducts water, dissolved nutrients, and organic compounds
2. stomata; allows for diffusion of gases, including water vapor, carbon dioxide, and oxygen
3. guard cells; controls opening and closing of a stoma
4. lower epidermis; protective covering on lower surface
5. spongy mesophyll; site of photosynthesis
6. palisade mesophyll; site of photosynthesis
7. upper epidermis; protective covering on upper surface
8. Adaptions include a broad surface to capture sunlight, cells filled with chloroplasts, air spaces in the spongy mesophyll for diffusion of gases, vascular tissue for conducting substances, and stomata for obtaining carbon dioxide.

Page 83
Structure and Function of a Flower

1. stamen; male reproductive structure
2. anther; produces pollen
3. filament; anchors or supports anther
4. pistil; female reproductive structure
5. stigma; traps pollen
6. style; anchors or supports stigma
7. ovary; site of egg production
8. sepal; outer covering
9. petal; colorful part of many plants that attracts insects

Page 84
Plants vs. Humans

1. stomata
2. xylem; phloem
3. usually roots
4. usually leaves
5. cell walls; wood
6. roots
7. mitochondria; chloroplasts

ANSWER KEY cont'd.

Unit 9
Page 88
Review

1. C
2. A
3. D
4. B
5. C
6. D

7. Most insects are small because their exoskeleton limits how large they can get.
8. In an open circulatory system, blood passes through open spaces. In a closed circulatory system, blood is always contained with a vessel, such as an artery, vein, or capillary.

Page 89
Hydra

1. A hydra displays radial symmetry as can be seen by the arrangement of its tentacles that branch out in all directions from a central point.
2. The illustration includes both a bud (asexual reproduction) and testis and ovary (sexual reproduction).
3. The tentacles capture food and then pass it down into the hydra's body cavity where it is digested.

Page 90
Earthworm

1. The digestive tube is enclosed by the elongated body tube.
2. The brain is located near the front. This is an advantage in that these segments are the first to come into contact with objects.
3. Oxygen and carbon dioxide diffuse through the earthworm's skin.

Page 91
Grasshopper

1. thorax: prothorax, mesothorax, and metathorax
2. antennae, simple eye, and compound eye
3. forewing, hindwing, walking legs (two pairs), and jumping legs

4. The spiracles are the openings through which gases involved in respiration diffuse.
5. exoskeleton
6. The forewing is leathery. This helps protect the membranous hindwings that are underneath.

Page 92
Classification II

1. E
2. D
3. B
4. A
5. C

Unit 10
Page 99
Review

1. A
2. D
3. A
4. C
5. D
6. B
7. B
8. C
9. endocrine and nervous systems
10. Answers can vary. One possibility includes the circulatory and excretory systems as evidenced by the relationship between the capillaries and a nephron, especially between the glomerulus and Bowman's capsule.

Page 100
The Circulatory System

1. right atrium
2. pulmonary vein
3. right ventricle
4. septum
5. left ventricle
6. pulmonary vein
7. left atrium
8. pulmonary artery
9. septum
10. Pulmonary veins are the only veins that carry oxygenated blood.
11. The walls of the ventricles are thicker because they must pump blood a greater distance than do the walls of the atria.
12. The pulmonary arteries that transport blood to the lungs carry deoxygenated blood.

Answer Key
Biology, SV 0423-9

ANSWER KEY cont'd.

Page 101

The Respiratory System Word Search

1. alveolus
2. carbon dioxide
3. larynx
4. oxygen
5. bronchus
6. diaphram
7. lung
8. pharynx
9. capillary
10. epiglottis
11. trachea
12. air
13. diffusion
14. breathing
15. nose

Page 102

Skeletal and Musclar Systems

1. J
2. A, H
3. I
4. C
5. D
6. C, D, E, F, H, J, K
7. A, I
8. K
9. B
10. B, G
11. E
12. A
13. fixed joint; Tendon, skeletal muscle, and arm bone are all involved in movement, unlike a fixed joint.
14. contracts and relaxes; Provides support, produces red blood cells, and stores minerals are all functions of the skeletal system, whereas contracts and relaxes applies to the muscular system.

Page 103

The Digestive System

1. mouth; grinds food and digests carbohydrates
2. liver; produces bile used for lipid digestion
3. anus; eliminates solid wastes
4. pharynx; passageway for food
5. esophagus; passageway for food
6. stomach; churns food and digests proteins
7. pancreas; produces digestive enzymes that enter small intestine
8. small intestine; completes digestive process and absorbs nutrients
9. large intestine; absorbs excess water and stores solid wastes

Answer Key
Biology, SV 0423-9

ANSWER KEY cont'd.

Page 104
The Excretory System
1. kidney
2. ureter
3. bladder
4. urethra
5. Bowman's capsule
6. loop of Henle
7. glomerulus
8. proximal convoluted tubule
9. distal convoluted tubule

Page 105
The Reproductive System
1. on or about day 14
2. luteinizing hormone
3. progesterone
4. The uterus thickens and develops more blood vessels.
5. The uterus sheds its thickened lining and blood vessels.
6. fertilization

Pages 106–107
The Endocrine System
1. glucagons and insulin directly; aldosterone, cortisol, and thyroxine are also involved by affecting carbohydrate metabolism
2. adrenal gland
3. Yes, because the pineal gland regulates sleep patterns.
4. pancreas
5. A malfunctioning thymus may make a person more prone to infection because white cells are affected.
6. The parathyroid glands decrease the calcium levels in the bones because they increase their levels in the bloodstream.
7. estrogen, progesterone, and androgens

8. Both systems are involved in homeostasis by coordinating various structures and activities.
9. Damage to the pituitary gland can affect the functioning of other endocrine glands.

Page 108
The Nervous System Crossword

Across
3. spinal cord
7. axon
8. nucleus
9. neuron
11. cerebellum
14. reflex

Down
1. cerebrum
2. tongue
3. synapse
4. involuntary
5. dendrite
6. muscle
10. chemical
12. brain
13. eye

CPSIA information can be obtained
at www.ICGtesting.com
Printed in the USA
BVHW011405130922
646898BV00012B/364